elevate science

SAVVAS
LEARNING COMPANY

AUTHORS

You're an author!

As you write in this science book, your answers and personal discoveries will be recorded for you to keep, making this book unique to you. That is why you are one of the primary authors of this book.

✎ **In the space below, print your name, school, town, and state. Then write a short autobiography that includes your interests and accomplishments.**

YOUR NAME ....

SCHOOL ....

TOWN, STATE ....

AUTOBIOGRAPHY ....

Your Photo

ISBN-13: 978-1-418-31053-0
ISBN-10: 1-418-31053-0

Program Authors

ZIPPORAH MILLER, Ed.D.
Coordinator for K-12 Science Programs, Anne Arundel County Public Schools
Dr. Zipporah Miller currently serves as the Senior Manager for Organizational Learning with the Anne Arundel County Public School System. Prior to that she served as the K-12 Coordinator for science in Anne Arundel County. She conducts national training to science stakeholders on the Next Generation Science Standards. Dr. Miller also served as the Associate Executive Director for Professional Development Programs and conferences at the National Science Teachers Association (NSTA) and served as a reviewer during the development of Next Generation Science Standards. Dr. Miller holds a doctoral degree from the University of Maryland College Park, a master's degree in school administration and supervision from Bowie State University and a bachelor's degree from Chadron State College.

MICHAEL J. PADILLA, Ph.D.
Professor Emeritus, Eugene P. Moore School of Education, Clemson University, Clemson, South Carolina
Michael J. Padilla taught science in middle and secondary schools, has more than 30 years of experience educating middle-school science teachers, and served as one of the writers of the 1996 U.S. National Science Education Standards. In recent years Mike has focused on teaching science to English Language Learners. His extensive experience as Principal Investigator on numerous National Science Foundation and U.S. Department of Education grants resulted in more than $35 million in funding to improve science education. He served as president of the National Science Teachers Association, the world's largest science teaching organization, in 2005–6.

MICHAEL E. WYSESSION, Ph.D
Professor of Earth and Planetary Sciences, Washington University, St. Louis, Missouri
Author of more than 100 science and science education publications, Dr. Wysession was awarded the prestigious National Science Foundation Presidential Faculty Fellowship and Packard Foundation Fellowship for his research in geophysics, primarily focused on using seismic tomography to determine the forces driving plate tectonics. Dr. Wysession is also a leader in geoscience literacy and education; he is the chair of the Earth Science Literacy Initiative, the author of several popular video lectures on geology in the *Great Courses* series, and a lead writer of the *Next Generation Science Standards**.

*Next Generation Science Standards is a registered trademark of WestEd. Neither WestEd nor the lead states and partners that developed the Next Generation Science Standards were involved in the production of this product, and do not endorse it. NGSS Lead States. 2013. *Next Generation Science Standards: For States, By States.* Washington, DC: The National Academies Press.

REVIEWERS

Program Consultants

Carol Baker
Science Curriculum

Dr. Carol K. Baker is superintendent for Lyons Elementary K-8 School District in Lyons, Illinois. Prior to this, she was Director of Curriculum for Science and Music in Oak Lawn, Illinois. Before this she taught Physics and Earth Science for 18 years. In the recent past, Dr. Baker also wrote assessment questions for ACT (EXPLORE and PLAN), was elected president of the Illinois Science Teachers Association from 2011–2013, and served as a member of the Museum of Science and Industry (Chicago) advisory board. She is a writer of the Next Generation Science Standards. Dr. Baker received her B.S. in Physics and a science teaching certification. She completed her master's of Educational Administration (K-12) and earned her doctorate in Educational Leadership.

Jim Cummins
ELL

Dr. Cummins's research focuses on literacy development in multilingual schools and the role technology plays in learning across the curriculum. *Elevate Science* incorporates research-based principles for integrating language with the teaching of academic content based on Dr. Cummins's work.

Elfrieda Hiebert
Literacy

Dr. Hiebert, a former primary-school teacher, is President and CEO of TextProject, a non-profit aimed at providing open-access resources for instruction of beginning and struggling readers, She is also a research associate at the University of California Santa Cruz. Her research addresses how fluency, vocabulary, and knowledge can be fostered through appropriate texts, and her contributions have been recognized through awards such as the Oscar Causey Award for Outstanding Contributions to Reading Research (Literacy Research Association, 2015), Research to Practice award (American Educational Research Association, 2013), and the William S. Gray Citation of Merit Award for Outstanding Contributions to Reading Research (International Reading Association, 2008).

Content Reviewers

Alex Blom, Ph.D.
Associate Professor
Department Of Physical Sciences
Alverno College
Milwaukee, Wisconsin

Joy Branlund, Ph.D.
Department of Physical Science
Southwestern Illinois College
Granite City, Illinois

Judy Calhoun
Associate Professor
Physical Sciences
Alverno College
Milwaukee, Wisconsin

Stefan Debbert
Associate Professor of Chemistry
Lawrence University
Appleton, Wisconsin

Diane Doser
Professor
Department of Geological Sciences
University of Texas at El Paso
El Paso, Texas

Rick Duhrkopf, Ph.D.
Department of Biology
Baylor University
Waco, Texas

Jennifer Liang
University of Minnesota Duluth
Duluth, Minnesota

Heather Mernitz, Ph.D.
Associate Professor of Physical Sciences
Alverno College
Milwaukee, Wisconsin

Joseph McCullough, Ph.D.
Cabrillo College
Aptos, California

Katie M. Nemeth, Ph.D.
Assistant Professor
College of Science and Engineering
University of Minnesota Duluth
Duluth, Minnesota

Maik Pertermann
Department of Geology
Western Wyoming Community College
Rock Springs, Wyoming

Scott Rochette
Department of the Earth Sciences
The College at Brockport
State University of New York
Brockport, New York

David Schuster
Washington University in St Louis
St. Louis, Missouri

Shannon Stevenson
Department of Biology
University of Minnesota Duluth
Duluth, Minnesota

Paul Stoddard, Ph.D.
Department of Geology and Environmental Geosciences
Northern Illinois University
DeKalb, Illinois

Nancy Taylor
American Public University
Charles Town, West Virginia

Teacher Reviewers

Rita Armstrong
Los Cerritos Middle School
Thousand Oaks, California

Tyler C. Britt, Ed.S.
Curriculum & Instructional
Practice Coordinator
Raytown Quality Schools
Raytown, Missouri

Holly Bowser
Barstow High School
Barstow, California

David Budai
Coachella Valley Unified School District
Coachella, California

A. Colleen Campos
Grandview High School
Aurora, Colorado

Jodi DeRoos
Mojave River Academy
Colton, California

Colleen Duncan
Moore Middle School
Redlands, California

Nicole Hawke
Westside Elementary
Thermal, California

Margaret Henry
Lebanon Junior High School
Lebanon, Ohio

Ashley Humphrey
Riverside Preparatory Elementary
Oro Grande, California

Adrianne Kilzer
Riverside Preparatory Elementary
Oro Grande, California

Danielle King
Barstow Unified School District
Barstow, California

Kathryn Kooyman
Riverside Preparatory Elementary
Oro Grande, California

Esther Leonard M.Ed. and L.M.T.
Gifted and Talented Implementation Specialist
San Antonio Independent School District
San Antonio, Texas

Diana M. Maiorca, M.Ed.
Los Cerritos Middle School
Thousand Oaks, California

Kevin J. Maser, Ed.D.
H. Frank Carey Jr/Sr High School
Franklin Square, New York

Corey Mayle
Brogden Middle School
Durham, North Carolina

Keith McCarthy
George Washington Middle School
Wayne, New Jersey

Rudolph Patterson
Cobalt Institute of Math and Science
Victorville, California

Yolanda O. Peña
John F. Kennedy Junior High School
West Valley City, Utah

Stacey Phelps
Mojave River Academy
Oro Grande, California

Susan Pierce
Bryn Mawr Elementary
Redlands Unified School District
Redlands, California

Cristina Ramos
Mentone Elementary School
Redlands Unified School District
Mentone, California

Mary Regis
Franklin Elementary School
Redlands, California

Bryna Selig
Gaithersburg Middle School
Gaithersburg, Maryland

Pat (Patricia) Shane, Ph.D.
STEM & ELA Education Consultant
Chapel Hill, North Carolina

Elena Valencia
Coral Mountain Academy
Coachella, California

Janelle Vecchio
Mission Elementary School
Redlands, California

Brittney Wells
Riverside Preparatory Elementary
Oro Grande, California

Kristina Williams
Sequoia Middle School
Newbury Park, California

Safety Reviewers

Douglas Mandt, M.S.
Science Education Consultant
Edgewood, Washington

Juliana Textley, Ph.D.
Author, NSTA books on school science safety
Adjunct Professor
Lesley University
Cambridge, Massachusetts

HANDS-ON LABS
uConnect
uInvestigate
uDemonstrate

California Spotlight

California's Changes Over Time

Go to SavvasRealize.com to access your digital course.

Elevate Science combines the best science narrative with a robust online program. Throughout the lessons, digital support is presented at point of use to enhance your learning experience.

Online Resources

Savvas Realize™ is your online science class. This digital-learning environment includes:

- Student eTEXT
- Instructor eTEXT
- Project-Based Learning
- Virtual Labs

- Interactivities
- Videos
- Assessments
- Study Tools
- and more!

Digital Features

 VIDEO

 INTERACTIVITY

 VIRTUAL LAB

 ASSESSMENT

 eTEXT

 APP

Keep an eye out for these **icons**, which indicate the different ways your textbook is enhanced online.

Digital activities are located throughout the narrative to deepen your understanding of scientific concepts.

 INTERACTIVITY

Interpret models of relationships in various ecosystems.

Elevate your thinking!

California Elevate Science takes science to a whole new level and lets you take ownership of your learning. Explore science in the world around you. Investigate how things work. Think critically and solve problems! *California Elevate Science* helps you think like a scientist, so you're ready for a world of discoveries.

Exploring California

California spotlights explore California phenomena. Topic Quests help connect lesson concepts together and reflect 3-dimensional learning.

- Science concepts organized around phenomena
- Topics weave together 3-D learning
- Engineering focused on solving problems and improving designs

Student Discourse

California Elevate Science promotes active discussion, higher order thinking and analysis and prepares you for high school through:

- High-level write-in prompts
- Evidence-based arguments
- Practice in speaking and writing

California Spotlight
Instructional Segment 2

Before the Topics
Identify the Problem

California Flood Management

Phenomenon In February of 2017, workers at the Orov...

Quest KICKOFF

How can you use solids, liquids, and gases to lift a car?

STEM Phenomenon Auto mechanics often need to go under cars to repair the parts in the under-carriage, such as the shocks and exhaust ...

Model It!

Crystalline and Amorphous Solids
Figure 5 A pat of butter is an amorphous solid. The particles that make up the butter are not arranged in a regular pattern. The sapphire gem stones are crystalline solids. Draw what you think the particles look like in a crystalline solid.

READING CHECK **Explain** In your own words, explain the main differences between crystalline solids and amorphous solids.

Quest CHECK-IN

In this lesson, you learned what happens to the particles of substances during melting, freezing, evaporation, boiling, condensation, and sublimation. You also thought about how thermal energy plays a role in these changes of state.

Predict Why do you need to take the temperature of the surroundings into consideration when designing a system with materials that can change state?

Academic Vocabulary

In orange juice, bits of pulp are suspended in liquid. Explain what you think *suspended* means.

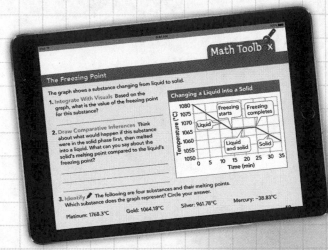

Build Literacy Skills

By connecting science to other disciplines like:

- Mathematics
- Reading and Writing
- STEM/Engineering

Focus on Inquiry

Case studies put you in the shoes of a scientist to solve real-world mysteries using real data. You will be able to:

- Analyze data
- Formulate claims
- Build evidence-based arguments

Enter the Digital Classroom

Virtual labs, 3-D expeditions, and dynamic videos take science beyond the classroom.

- Open-ended virtual labs
- Google Expeditions and field trips
- NBC Learn videos

How have living populations changed over time in response to environmental changes?

Explore It

Look at the picture. What do you observe? What questions do you have about the phenomenon? Write your observations and questions in the space below.

California Spotlight

MS-LS4-1, MS-LS4-2, MS-LS4-4,
MS-LS4-6, EP&CIIa, EP&CIIc

Inquiry

- How do specific traits help organisms access or utilize resources more efficiently?
- How does a population benefit from having diversity within it?
- In what ways are humans similar to dinosaurs?
- How do rocks tell us about the history of life?

Topic

9 Natural Selection and Change Over Time

During the Cambrian Period, the land that now makes up California was not yet part of North America. The area that now makes up the White-Inyo mountain range along the border of California and Nevada near Bishop was once covered by a shallow sea.

Before the Topic
Identify the Problem

California's Changes Over Time

Phenomenon Californians are always on the move. And so is the ground beneath their feet. Over millions of years, the land that makes up California has changed both its position on Earth and its location relative to the rest of what is now North America.

The oldest rock in the state dates from about 1.7 billion years ago. Life started to appear in what is now California about 570 million years ago, during the Cambrian Period.

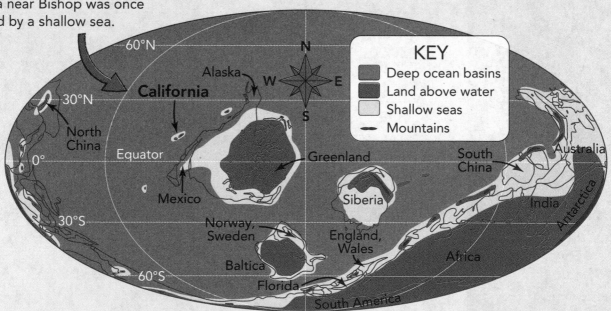

Changes in Rocks

Earth's surface is always changing. Land is constantly forged and destroyed by forces in the rock cycle, shifting tectonic plates, and other system processes. The fossil record indicates that California's present location and composition are the result of geological changes to the Earth's surface. While California's oldest rocks do not contain fossils, some younger rocks contain fossils from marine organisms. The fossils found in these rocks provide evidence to scientists that parts of California could have once been parts of former oceanic plates that collided into a continental plate. Rock record evidence reveals that volcanic activity and continental sediments formed much of California's land.

Today, many different types of rock make up the land that is California. Each rock type was made during a different period in Earth's history. Recent research finds that the rock cycle, particularly changes in the Earth's crust, played a key role in the start of life on the planet. Without these changes, complex life forms could not have developed on Earth.

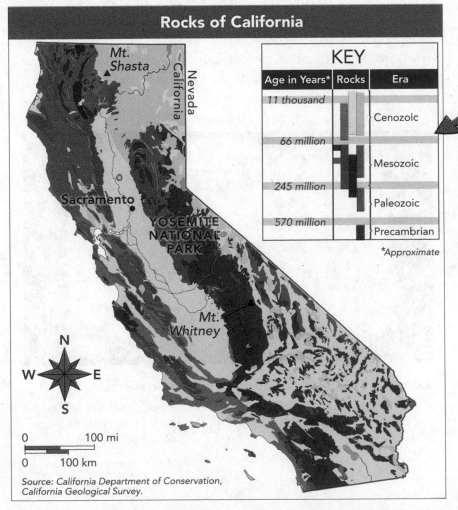

The color-coded time scale shows the age of different rocks that make up California today.

SEP Analyze Data
Where would you most likely find rocks with no fossils? Look for patterns in the map to identify and circle the location.

3

The Great Oxidation Event

In order for life to develop on Earth, oxygen was needed in Earth's atmosphere. It took geological and biological changes to kick-start a process (around 2.3 billion years ago) that increased levels of oxygen in the atmosphere. This dramatic rise in atmospheric oxygen is known as "the great oxidation event." The increased supply of atmospheric oxygen led to an explosion in the number and diversity of species. It also made it possible for organisms to adapt to life on land.

Some of the oldest known fossils are around 3.5 billion years old and show the presence of cyanobacteria. These bacteria were unicellular organisms that produced oxygen as a by-product of photosynthesis. Until recently, scientists could not explain why oxygen levels did not increase for another billion years. Research reveals that a rock-forming mineral, olivine, could have been the reason.

Olivine is one of Earth's most abundant minerals. Olivine traps oxygen when it reacts with water. So some scientists have speculated that olivine in the land covered by shallow seas would have absorbed the oxygen that cyanobacteria would have produced. As the composition of Earth's continental surface rocks changed, however, olivine was replaced by other rocks. With less olivine present, oxygen built up in the oceans and atmosphere.

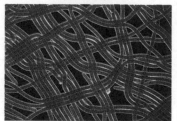

Meet the kick-starters of Earth's atmosphere—olivine (top) and cyanobacteria, better known as blue-green algae (bottom). Rocks with olivine are mined in the Klamath Mountains that run from northern California into Orgeon. Fossils of cyanobacteria can be found in the White-Inyo Mountain range.

Archaeocyatha, a type of ancient sponge, appeared around 530 million years ago. Before going extinct, they evolved into hundreds of different species, many of which were Earth's first reef-builders.

1. **Identify** 🖊 Circle the fossil of an Archaeocyatha.
2. **SEP Construct Explanations** Why would reef-building be important for life on Earth and in the ancient land mass that would become California?

....

....

....

Changes in Life Forms

California is rich in fossils. They reveal the amazing variety of species that once lived in California. The fossils reveal how different species have adapted over time as conditions changed. Many animals that once roamed through California now exist only in the form of fossils. The Mojave Desert, for example, contains fossils of ancient horses, ancient elephants, and camels. While many species that once lived in California disappeared from the land mass that become North America, some animals managed to migrate and thrive on other continents.

California's state fossil, the saber-toothed cat (*Smilodon*), was common in California around 2.5 million years ago but went extinct, disappearing around 10,000 years ago. The excavation site at the La Brea Tar Pits in Los Angeles contains many of their fossils, evidence that there was once a sizable population of these ancient cats in California.

All sorts of animals that lived in California during the last Ice Age met their demise in the La Brea Tar Pits: ancient horses, camels, ground sloths, jaguars, mammoths, and saber-toothed cats.

Saber-toothed cats were predators weighing up to 350 kg (770 lbs).

Explain Phenomena What are some environmental conditions that the saber-toothed cat may not have been adapted for that could have caused its extinction?

....

....

....

....

Adapting to Climate Change

Throughout this segment, you will learn about how organisms adapt to their surroundings and how species change over time. You will also explore how humans have influenced the evolution of some species on the planet. Understanding these processes helps scientists see how the interrelationships between Earth's systems and processes can affect evolution and the diversity of life. In the topics in this segment, you will investigate the factors that drive evolutionary changes in animals and plants.

A team of scientists, including researchers from the University of California at Riverside, recently discovered a relationship between climate change and evolution. They found that an extreme climate event in the past drastically increased oxygen levels in Earth's ocean-atmosphere system. That event was the thawing of "Snowball Earth." Analyzing trace elements in rocks provided the team with strong evidence for an oxygen spike after a period of thawing. The fossil record further provided evidence of a sudden increase in biodiversity. Because of the thawing, there was an explosion of algae and then small animal life forms.

Snowball Earth refers to a few brief periods 650–900 million years ago when ice covered most of the planet's surface.

Leatherback sea turtles lay their eggs in Indonesia and then swim thousands of miles to their feeding grounds along California's coast. Jellyfish, their main food source, thrive in the upwelling of cooler waters around California.

CCC Stability and Change Consider how a severe climate event that causes water temperatures to increase might affect the leatherback sea turtle.

....

....

....

....

What questions can you ask to help you make sense of this phenomena?

Natural Selection and Change Over Time

Investigative Phenomenon

What kinds of data and evidence explain how characteristics of organisms change over time?

MS-LS3-1 Develop and use a model to describe why structural changes to genes (mutations) located on chromosomes may affect proteins and may result in harmful, beneficial, or neutral effects to the structure and function of the organism.

MS-LS4-1 Analyze and interpret data for patterns in the fossil record that document the existence, diversity, extinction, and change of life forms throughout the history of life on Earth under the assumption that natural laws operate today as in the past.

MS-LS4-2 Apply scientific ideas to construct an explanation for the anatomical similarities and differences among modern organisms and between modern and fossil organisms to infer evolutionary relationships.

MS-LS4-3 Analyze displays of pictorial data to compare patterns of similarities in the embryological development across multiple species to identify relationships not evident in the fully formed anatomy.

MS-LS4-4 Construct an explanation based on evidence that describes how genetic variations of traits in a population increase some individuals' probability of surviving and reproducing in a specific environment.

MS-LS4-5 Gather and synthesize information about the technologies that have changed the way humans influence the inheritance of desired traits in organisms.

MS-LS4-6 Use mathematical representations to support explanations of how natural selection may lead to increases and decreases of specific traits in populations over time.

EP&CIIa Students should be developing an understanding that the direct and indirect changes to natural systems due to the growth of human populations and their consumption rates influence the geographic extent, composition, biological diversity, and viability of natural systems.

EP&CIIc Students should be developing an understanding that the expansion and operation of human communities influences the geographic extent, composition, biological diversity, and viability of natural systems.

Has this dragonfly changed from its fossilized ancestor?

HANDS-ON LAB

uConnect Analyze evidence that whales may have walked on land.

What questions do you have about the phenomenon?

Quest PBL

A Migration Puzzle

Figure It Out To understand how bird populations change over time in response to environmental conditions, ornithologists (scientists who study birds) analyze long-term data. In this problem-based Quest activity, you will investigate factors that may be influencing changes in two populations of European blackcaps. By applying what you learn from each lesson, digital activity, and hands-on lab, you will determine what is causing the changes to the bird populations. Then in the Findings activity, you will prepare a multimedia report to communicate what you have learned and to explain the changes in the blackcap populations.

 **INTERACTIVITY**

A Migration Puzzle

 MS-LS3-1, MS-LS4-1, MS-LS4-2, MS-LS4-4, MS-LS4-5, MS-LS4-6, EP&CIIa, EP&CIIc

NBC LEARN ▶ VIDEO

After watching the Quest Kickoff video about migrating golden eagles, list some of the factors that might affect the birds' migration patterns and routes.

....

....

....

....

....

....

....

....

....

Quest CHECK-IN

IN LESSON 1
What differences exist between the UK and Spanish blackcaps? Determine evidence for variations in the European blackcap populations.

 INTERACTIVITY

Meet the Blackcaps

IN LESSON 2
What are the roles of genes and mutations in natural selection? Think about how you can include these factors in your report.

Quest CHECK-IN

IN LESSON 3
How can natural selection and inherited variations influence a population? Investigate factors that may have caused the variations in the European blackcaps.

 INTERACTIVITY

Evolution of the Blackcaps

In the 1960s, some European blackcaps started migrating to the United Kingdom from Central Europe during the winter. Over time, they have formed a distinct population of blackcaps.

IN LESSON 4

What can you learn from the fossil record? Think about how the fossil record of the European blackcap might provide information on how the bird has adapted over time.

Quest CHECK-IN

IN LESSON 5

What else would be helpful to know about European blackcaps? Research your questions and gather information to include in your report.

INTERACTIVITY

Prepare Your Report

Quest FINDINGS

Complete the Quest!

Create a multimedia report about the two populations of European blackcaps and what caused them to be so different from each other.

INTERACTIVITY

Reflect on Blackcap Migration

1.1

HANDS-ON LAB

uInvestigate Model how species change over time.

MS-LS4-4 Construct an explanation based on evidence that describes how genetic variations of traits in a population increase some individuals' probability of surviving and reproducing in a specific environment.

Connect It !

✏ **Draw an arrow pointing to the squirrel that you think is better suited for the environment.**

SEP Construct Explanations Why do you think that squirrel is better suited for the environment? Explain your reasoning.

....

....

....

....

Observing Changes

Suppose you put a birdfeeder outside your kitchen or classroom window. You enjoy watching birds and gray squirrels come to get a free meal. The squirrels seem to be perfectly skilled at climbing the feeder and breaking open seeds. One day, you are surprised to see a white squirrel, like the squirrel in **Figure 1**, visiting the feeder. This new white squirrel and the gray squirrel appear to be the same species—a group of similar organisms that can mate with each other and produce offspring that can also mate and reproduce. You would probably have a few questions about where this squirrel came from and why it is white!

Curiosity About How Life Changes Scientists such as Charles Darwin were also curious about the differences they observed in natural populations. A variation is any difference between individuals of the same species. Some scientists asked how life on Earth got started and how it has changed over time throughout the planet's history. The scientists wondered what dinosaurs were like and why they disappeared. Darwin and others worked to develop a theory of evolution—the process by which modern organisms have descended from ancient organisms.

INTERACTIVITY

Explore feeding adaptations of animals in a coral reef ecosystem.

Surprise at the Birdfeeder!
Figure 1 In Brevard, North Carolina, about one-third of the Eastern gray squirrel population is white. In 1949, a resident received a pair of white squirrels as a gift. When one squirrel escaped, the other was released to join its friend. Soon after, people began to spot more white squirrels in town.

Organizing Life

Figure 2 Linnaeus classified life based on the structures of each organism.

Classify ✐ Identify three characteristics that you can observe in the image and list them below. Assign each characteristic a shape: a circle, rectangle, or triangle. Using the characteristics you have identified, organize the organisms in the image into three groups by drawing the appropriate shapes around them.

....

....

....

....

....

....

....

....

....

Make Meaning What problem or question have you had that required you to make observations and gather evidence to figure it out?

Linnaeus' System of Classification

Carolus Linnaeus (1707–1778) developed the first scientific system for classifying and naming living things. Linnaeus collected samples of organisms from around the world. When classifying the organisms according to shared characteristics like those shown in **Figure 2**, he observed that there were variations of traits within a species. He was able to describe the variations and diversity of life, but not explain what caused that variation and diversity. No one was yet exploring how organisms came to be the way they are. In fact, many people still believed that organisms could appear out of the air as if by magic.

Lamarck's Idea

The first serious attempts to explain evolution began in the late 1700s. A French scientist, Jean-Baptiste Lamarck (1744–1829), was put in charge of a museum department of "Insects and Worms," which also included all the invertebrates, or animals without backbones. Lamarck devoted himself to learning everything he could about invertebrates. Unlike Linnaeus, Lamarck wasn't satisfied with describing what the animals looked like. Instead, Lamarck attempted to figure out how the organisms came to be. After much study, Lamarck developed the first attempt at a scientific hypothesis explaining how species change over time.

Lamarck's Hypothesis of Transformation Lamarck mistakenly believed that organisms could change their traits by selectively using or not using various parts of their bodies. For example, moles could develop long, strong claws by digging through dirt. Lamarck **hypothesized** that if two adult moles with long claws mated, their offspring would inherit those claws, as shown in **Figure 3**. In the next generation, the individuals who used their claws more would pass even longer claws on to their offspring. In this way, the whole population of moles would gradually grow bigger, stronger claws, until they reached the form we see today.

Lamarck's transformation hypothesis doesn't support a consistent pattern for other traits when investigated further. It doesn't explain how features such as eyes could have developed. The hypothesis also does not work when tested with experiments. For example, you can force a plant to grow sideways. However, the offspring of the plant grow straight up toward the light. While his hypothesis was not supported, Lamarck did contribute some important new ideas. First, he suggested that a change in a species takes place by small, gradual steps. Second, he proposed that simple organisms could develop over many generations into more complex organisms.

Academic Vocabulary

Hypothesize comes from the Greek word for *foundation*. To hypothesize means to propose a hypothesis—a possible explanation to a question that can be investigated. A hypothesis can be based on limited evidence. Why is it helpful to hypothesize in subjects like history and science?

....

....

....

....

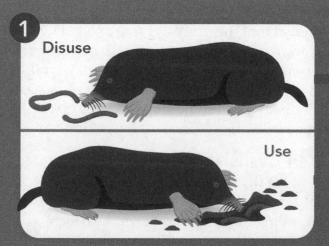

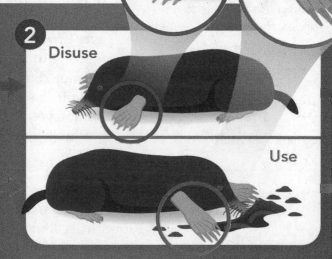

Lamarck's Transformation Hypothesis
Figure 3 🖊 In the open space, draw what you think the offspring of the mole that did not dig for food will look like, based on Lamarck's hypothesis.

☑ **CHECK POINT** Determine Conclusions Why was Lamarck's hypothesis not accepted?

....

....

....

3

Disuse

Use

Reading the Past

Figure 4 Charles Lyell discovered how to read Earth's history from layers of rock. Meanwhile, Mary Anning used fossils to reconstruct ancient animals.

1. Interpret Photos Examine the fossil. List the parts of the animal that you recognize. What kind of animal do you think this was?

....

....

....

2. CCC Identify Patterns Would you expect to find older or newer fossils in rock layers closer to the surface? Why?

....

....

....

....

....

Charles Lyell's Rocks

Not long after Lamarck proposed his ideas, a young lawyer named Charles Lyell (1797–1875) began studying naturally-formed layers of rocks and fossils, like those in **Figure 4**. A **fossil** is the preserved remains or traces of an organism that lived in the past. Lyell concluded that the features of Earth had changed a great deal over time. He also stated that the processes that created land features in the past were still active. Before Lyell, some people estimated that the world was less than 6,000 years old. Lyell and other scientists pushed that estimate back more than 300 million years. Lyell's discoveries set the stage for a theory of gradual evolution, or evolution over long periods of time.

Mary Anning's Fossils

Mary Anning (1799–1847) lived a much different life than Linnaeus, Lamarck, or Lyell. Coming from a poor family that made money by collecting fossils, Mary Anning would roam up and down the beach while searching for fossils in the steep cliffs along the English Channel. Anning taught herself how to reconstruct the bodies of fossilized animals. Many of these animals had never before been seen. Because of Anning's work, scientists began to realize that some animals had lived in the ancient past but no longer existed. While Anning had no formal training as a scientist, her observations and discoveries made her a key contributor in the study of both fossils and geology.

✓ **CHECK POINT** **Summarize Text** How did the scientists show that organisms and Earth changed over time?

....

....

Darwin's Journey

In 1831, 22-year-old Charles Darwin set out on a five-year trip around the world aboard a British navy ship, the HMS *Beagle*. Darwin was a naturalist—a person who observes and studies the natural world. The captain of the *Beagle* wanted someone aboard who could make and record observations as the crew explored South America. One of Darwin's professors suggested inviting Darwin. And thus was launched a brilliant career!

Darwin was surprised to see the diversity of living things he encountered during the voyage. He saw insects that looked like flowers. He also saw armadillos digging insects from the ground. These mammals with a leathery shell that looks like a small suit of armor would have been very strange creatures to see. Today, scientists know that organisms are even more diverse than Darwin thought. Scientists have calculated that there are millions of species on Earth—and new ones are being identified all the time. Scientists have no way to estimate how many undiscovered species exist, but they believe the numbers are very high.

Fossils On his journey aboard the *Beagle*, Darwin also saw fossils of animals that had died long ago. Some of the fossils he observed confused him. **Figure 5** shows fossils Darwin found that resembled the bones of living armadillos but were much larger in size. Darwin wondered what had happened to the ancient, giant armadillos. Over long periods of time, could the giant armadillos have evolved into the smaller species we see today?

Armored Animals

Figure 5 Darwin thought that the fossil bones of giant Glyptodons (right) resembled the bones of modern armadillos (left).

1. Determine Similarities List two common features that the animals share.

....

....

2. Infer Why might these features be important to both ancient and modern armadillos?

....

....

....

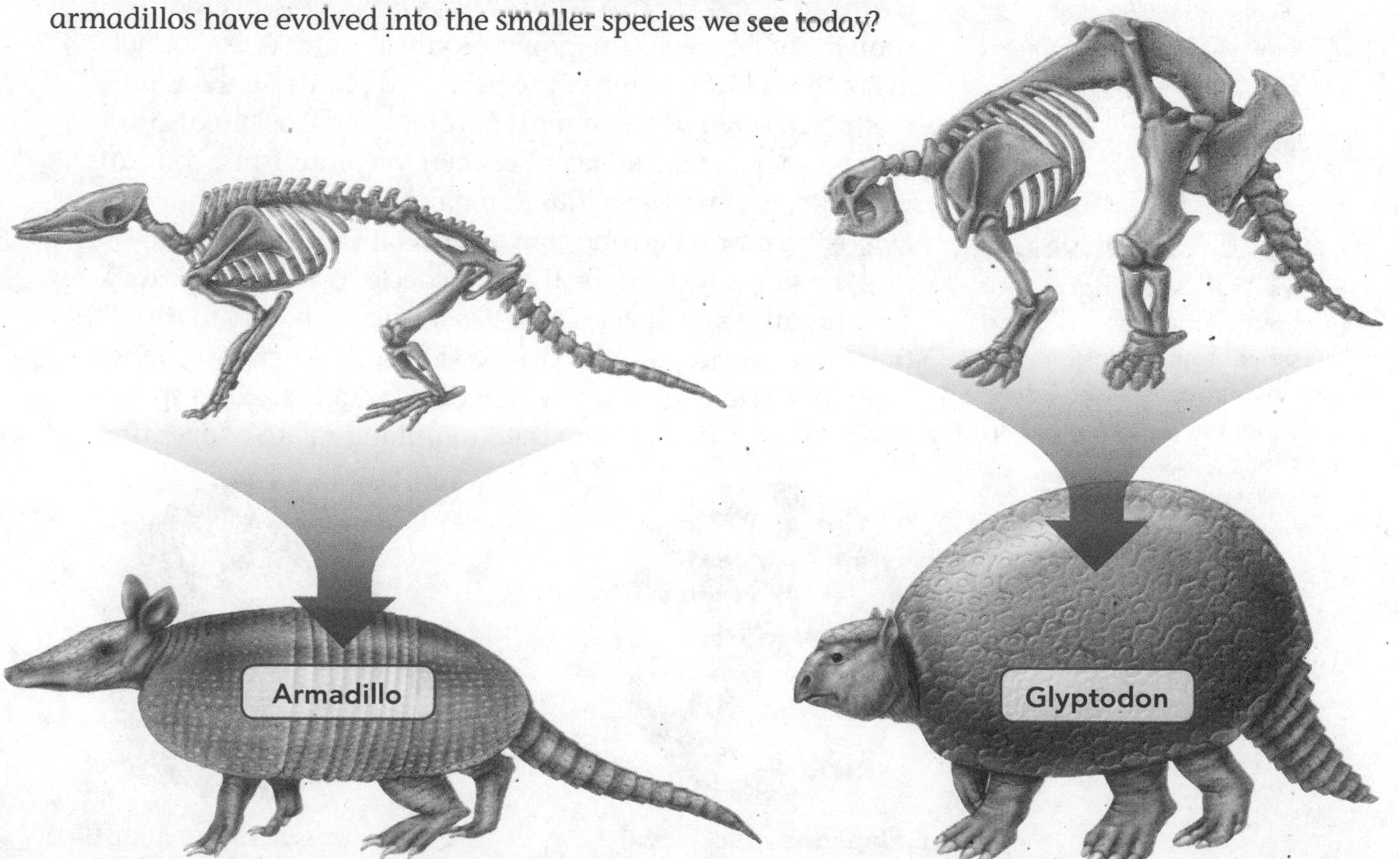

Armadillo

Glyptodon

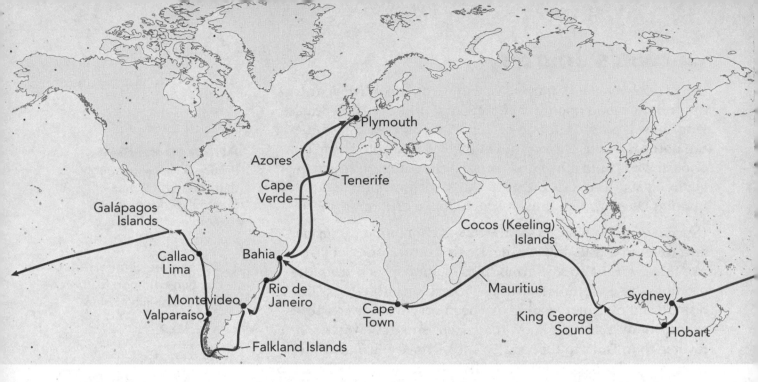

Voyage of the HMS *Beagle*, 1831–1836

Figure 6 Darwin sailed 40,000 miles around the world during his five-year voyage.

INTERACTIVITY

Observe organisms that Darwin encountered in the Galápagos Islands.

Long-Lost Relatives?

Figure 7 🖊 Mockingbirds on the South American mainland are similar to mockingbirds on the Galápagos Islands. Circle and label the features that are not similar.

CCC Relate Structure and Function Why do you think these birds have different traits?

....
....
....
....

Galápagos Organisms

The *Beagle* sailed to many different locations, as shown in **Figure 6**, and made several stops along the coast of South America. From what is now Peru on the Pacific coast, the ship traveled west to the Galápagos Islands. Darwin observed many different life forms there. He compared organisms from the Galápagos Islands to organisms that lived elsewhere. He also compared organisms living on the different islands.

Comparisons to the Mainland

Darwin discovered similarities between Galápagos organisms and those found in South America. Some of the birds and plants on the islands resembled those on the mainland. However, Darwin also noted important differences between the organisms. You can see differences between island and mainland mockingbirds in **Figure 7**. Darwin became convinced that species do not always stay the same. Instead, he thought species could change and even produce new species over time. Darwin began to think that the island species might be related to South American species. After much reflection, Darwin realized that the island species had become different from their mainland relatives over time.

Galápagos mockingbird

South American mockingbird

Comparisons Among the Islands Darwin collected birds from several of the Galápagos Islands. The birds were a little different from one island to the next. Darwin would learn that the birds were all types of finches. He concluded that the finch species were all related to a single common ancestor species that came from the mainland. Over time, different finches developed different beak shapes and sizes that were well suited to the food they ate. Beak shape is an example of an <mark>adaptation</mark>—an inherited behavior or physical characteristic that helps an organism survive and reproduce in its environment. Look at **Figure 8**. Birds with narrow, prying beaks can grasp insects. Those with long, pointed, sharp beaks can pick at cacti. Short, hooked beaks tear open fruit, while short, wide beaks crush seeds.

☑ CHECK POINT **Determine Central Ideas** What convinced Darwin that species can change over time?

....

....

Galápagos Finches
Figure 8 Darwin observed beak adaptations.

1. **Claim** Why is it necessary for finches to have different beaks?

....

....

....

....

2. **Evidence** ✏ Draw an arrow from each finch matching it to the type of food you think it eats.

3. **Reasoning** Explain why your evidence supports your claim.

....

....

....

....

....

....

....

Question It!

We Got the Beak!
SEP Construct Explanations The finches in **Figure 8** show variations due to adaptation. Suppose someone asks what could cause a species' beak to change. How would you answer the person?

....

....

....

....

....

19

INTERACTIVITY

Identify plant and animal adaptations and how they help the organisms survive.

VIDEO

Watch a video about the early study of evolution.

Literacy Connection

Determine Central Ideas
As you read, underline the elements that are needed to develop a scientific theory.

HANDS-ON LAB

Investigate Model how species change over time.

Darwin's Hypothesis Darwin thought about what he had observed during his voyage on the *Beagle*. By this time, while Darwin was convinced that organisms change over time, he wanted to know how the organisms changed. Darwin consulted other scientists and gathered more information. Based on his observations, Darwin reasoned that plants or animals that arrived on the Galápagos Islands faced conditions different from those on the nearby mainland. Darwin hypothesized that species change over many generations and become better adapted to new conditions. Darwin's hypothesis was an idea that contributed important new knowledge. Later, he and other scientists used it to test and develop a scientific theory.

Developing a Theory In science, a theory explains why and how things happen in nature. A scientific theory is a well-tested explanation for a wide range of observations and experimental results. Based on a body of facts, scientific theory is confirmed repeatedly through observation and experimentation. Darwin's ideas are often referred to as the theory of evolution. From the evidence he collected, and from all the discoveries of the scientists who had come before him, Darwin concluded that organisms on the Galápagos Islands had changed over time, or evolved.

✓ **CHECK POINT** **Cite Textual Evidence** Why do you think theories, like Darwin's theory of evolution, are important to science?

....

....

....

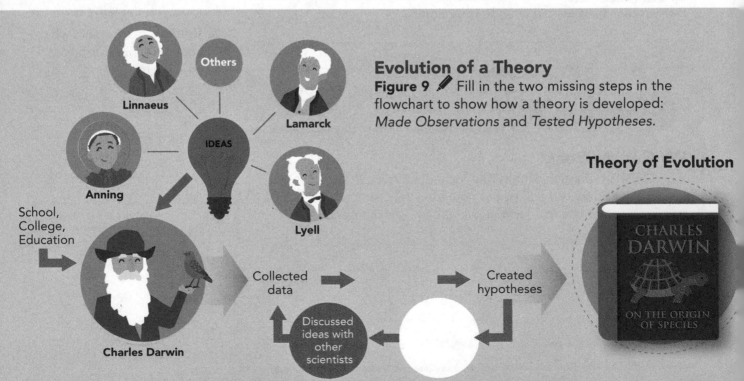

Evolution of a Theory
Figure 9 ✏ Fill in the two missing steps in the flowchart to show how a theory is developed: *Made Observations* and *Tested Hypotheses*.

Linnaeus

Others

Lamarck

IDEAS

Anning

Lyell

School, College, Education

Charles Darwin

Collected data

Discussed ideas with other scientists

Created hypotheses

Theory of Evolution

CHARLES DARWIN

ON THE ORIGIN OF SPECIES

☑ LESSON 1 Check

1. **Identify** Name four people, other than Darwin, whose work contributed to the study of evolution.

....

2. **Apply Scientific Reasoning** Why are fossils important to developing a theory of evolution?

....

....

....

....

3. **Compare and Contrast** How are variations and adaptations similar? How are they different?

....

....

....

....

....

....

4. **Integrate Information** Which two ideas of Lamarck contributed the most to Darwin's theory of evolution?

....

....

....

....

....

5. **SEP Construct Explanations** If the finches on the Galápagos Islands had such different beaks, how could Darwin think they shared a common ancestor from the mainland?

....

....

....

....

....

....

....

Quest CHECK-IN

In this lesson, you learned about adaptations and variations as well as the people whose ideas and activities contributed to understanding how organisms change over time. You also learned how Darwin developed his theory of evolution.

CCC Stability and Change Consider what you learned about variation and how species change over time. Why is it important to understand how a different migration route might be affecting the blackcaps' physical traits?

....

....

....

....

👆 INTERACTIVITY

Meet the Blackcaps

Go online to draw conclusions about the variations between the two groups, based on what you've learned about where the birds migrate in winter.

HANDS-ON LAB

uInvestigate Measure variation in plant and animal populations.

MS-LS4-4 Construct an explanation based on evidence that describes how genetic variations of traits in a population increase some individuals' probability of surviving and reproducing in a specific environment.

MS-LS4-5 Gather and synthesize information about the technologies that have changed the way humans influence the inheritance of desired traits in organisms.

MS-LS4-6 Use mathematical representations to support explanations of how natural selection may lead to increases and decreases of specific traits in populations over time.

Connect It !

✏️ **Estimate how many dead fish are shown here. Write your estimation on the photograph.**

Explain Phenomena Some fish survived this event, known as a fish kill. What might be different about the fish that survived?

....

....

Apply Scientific Reasoning If low oxygen levels occur every year and cause fish kills, how might the population of fish change over time?

....

Evolution by Natural Selection

Living in a small body of water can be dangerous for fish. If water conditions become unhealthy, there is nowhere for the fish to go. Too little rain, too many fish, and an overgrowth of algae can work together to reduce oxygen levels in water. **Figure 1** shows what happened when oxygen levels fell too low. A "fish kill" can wipe out most of the local population of a species of fish. Some individuals, however, usually survive the disaster. These fish will live to reproduce, thus ensuring the species survives.

Darwin's Search for a Mechanism After his return to England, Darwin was not satisfied with his theory of evolution. He struggled to determine evolution's mechanism. A <mark>mechanism</mark> is the natural process by which something takes place. Darwin asked himself how organisms could change over time. And how could a species become better adapted to new conditions? To solve this mystery, Darwin performed experiments and read the works of other naturalists and scientists.

INTERACTIVITY

Investigate how a species of butterflyfish adapts to changes in its environment.

Fish Kill

Figure 1 Fish can survive only in water with dissolved oxygen. When oxygen levels fall too low, thousands of fish can perish at once.

Rock pigeon
(*Columba livia*)

Fantail pigeon

Silky fantail pigeon

Fancy Pigeons

Figure 2 Through artificial selection, Darwin helped to create the fantail pigeon (center) from the wild rock pigeon (left). Silky fantails (right) were then bred from the fantail pigeon. Despite their physical differences, these two breeds belong to the same species as the rock pigeon, *Columba livia*.

Make Observations List the differences you see between the three different pigeon types.

📓 Write About It

Farmers often selectively breed farm animals. When farmers breed and care for farm animals with certain genetic traits that humans desire, it is called animal husbandry. Write about how animal husbandry affects society. Consider farmers, restaurants, grocery stores, consumers, and the use of land resources.

Literacy Connection

Cite Textual Evidence As you read about natural selection, underline sentences or parts of sentences that you can refer to later to help you support your explanations about this process.

Artificial Selection Darwin studied farm and pet animals produced by artificial selection. In artificial selection, humans have the capacity to influence certain characteristics of organisms by breeding them selectively. Organisms with a desired parental trait, such as color, are bred by humans who calculate the probability of offspring inheriting the trait. Darwin himself bred pigeons with large, fan-shaped tails (**Figure 2**). He repeatedly allowed only those pigeons with many tail feathers to mate. In this way, Darwin produced pigeons with two or three times the usual number of tail feathers. Darwin thought that a process similar to artificial selection might happen in nature. But he wondered what natural process resulted in the selection.

Natural Selection Darwin understood how evolution could work when he read an essay by Thomas Malthus. Malthus noted that both animals and humans can produce many offspring. If all the offspring survived, the world would quickly become overpopulated. There would not be enough food for everyone, and part of the population would starve. Darwin realized that some individuals have traits that help them to survive and reproduce. If these traits are hereditary, they can be passed on to the next generation. Gradually, over many generations, more and more individuals will have the helpful traits.

The Origin of Species Darwin waited a long time to publish his ideas. He thought they might be too revolutionary for the public to accept. Then, in 1858, Alfred Russel Wallace sent Darwin a letter. Wallace had also read Malthus' work and discovered the same mechanism for evolution! The next year, Darwin published his theory in *The Origin of Species*. In his book, Darwin proposed that evolution occurs by means of natural selection, a process by which individuals that are better adapted to their environment are more likely to survive and reproduce than other members of the same species.

How Natural Selection Works
Darwin identified three factors that affect the process of natural selection: overproduction, variation, and competition. First, there must be overproduction, shown in **Figure 3** below. Darwin knew that most species produce more offspring than can possibly survive. Secondly, there must be variation. Members of a population differ from one another in many of their traits. For example, sea turtles may differ in color, size, the ability to crawl quickly on sand, and shell hardness. Such variations are hereditary, passed from parents to offspring through genetic material. Finally, there must be competition—the struggle among living things to get the necessary amount of food, water, and shelter. In many species, so many offspring are produced that there are not enough resources—food, water, and living space—for all of them.

✓ CHECK POINT **Summarize** What are the factors that affect the process of natural selection?

....

HANDS-ON LAB

U**Investigate** Measure variation in plant and animal populations.

Overproduction
Figure 3 Brown rats can give birth up to 12 times each year with about 6 to 11 pups in each litter. The young rats are ready to breed when they are 12 weeks old.

1. **SEP Analyze Data** About how many pups can each female rat produce every year?

....

2. **Draw Conclusions** Why can't every rat survive and reproduce at its maximum rate?

....

....

....

....

....

....

....

Selection Darwin observed that some traits make individuals better adapted to their environment. Those individuals were more likely to survive and reproduce, and their offspring would inherit the helpful trait. The offspring, in turn, would be more likely to survive and reproduce and pass the trait to their offspring. After many generations, the proportion of this helpful trait increases in the population. This is called *predominance* of that trait. The proportion of less helpful traits tends to decrease, a process called *suppression*. **Figure 4** illustrates how conditions in the environment select sea turtles with helpful traits to become parents of the next generation. Darwin proposed that, over a long time, natural selection can lead to change.

Adaptations and Selection

Figure 4 Once sea turtles hatch from a nest, they must be fast and strong enough to reach the ocean before predators arrive.

☑ CHECK POINT **Cite Textual Evidence** How is Darwin's proposal that natural selection can lead to change in a species supported in nature?

....

....

....

Math Toolbox

Hatching for Success

Sea turtles play an important role in maintaining Florida's coastal ecosystem.

1. **Graph Proportional Relationships** ✏ Complete the graph to compare the total number of sea turtle nests at each beach to the number of nests that hatched sea turtles. Create a key next to the graph.

2. **SEP Construct an Explanation** On which beach(es) would you create a turtle refuge? Cite evidence to support your response.

....

....

....

Beach	Total Nests	Hatched Nests
Barefoot Beach	174	50
City of Naples	148	14
Delnor Wiggins	46	6
Marco Island	52	15
10,000 Islands	87	13

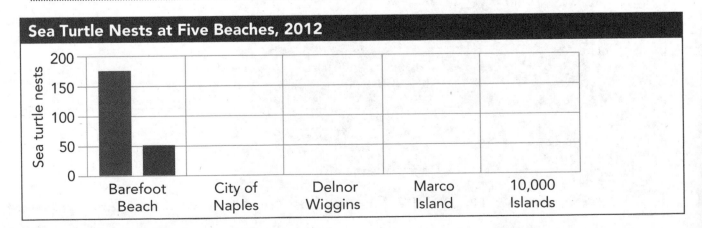

Sea Turtle Nests at Five Beaches, 2012

Environmental Change A change in the environment can affect an organism's ability to survive and may therefore lead to natural selection. For example, a storm can topple many trees in a forest. Trees that are better able to withstand strong winds have a survival advantage. In **Figure 5** you can see how natural selection might result in a shift in the population toward storm-resistant trees.

Natural Selection in Action

Figure 5 Natural events can lead to selection for favorable traits in a population. Read each image caption and use evidence to answer each question.

1990: Biologists survey a forest.

SEP Use Models List your observations related to the variation, competition, and overproduction of this tree population.

....

....

....

1991: Same forest after a windstorm.

Explain Phenomena What helpful trait did most of the surviving trees have?

....

....

....

2010: Same forest is surveyed again.

Make Observations How is the population different now compared to 1990?

....

....

2017: Another windstorm hits.

SEP Develop Models 🖉 In the space provided, draw the effect of the storm on the forest.

SEP Construct Explanations How will natural selection have changed the forest from 1990 to 2030?

....

....

INTERACTIVITY

Analyze data on how a mouse population changes.

 **VIRTUAL LAB**

Investigate how natural selection affects population traits over time.

Genes and Natural Selection Darwin did a brilliant job of explaining natural selection, but he was never able to figure out where variations come from. He also did not understand how traits were passed from parents to offspring. Darwin hypothesized that tiny particles from around the parents' bodies passed into the developing offspring. Even at the time, Darwin realized that this explanation was flawed. Yet he did not have enough information to formulate a better explanation. Recall Gregor Mendel and his study of heredity and genetics. Mendel's experiments in plant breeding took place during Darwin's life. His work showed that parents pass genes to their offspring. Genes are units of genetic material that provide instructions for a specific protein or function. Inherited variations result from individuals having different combinations of genes, as shown in **Figure 6**. Your hair color, eye color—and dimples, if you have them—are all determined by the genes your parents passed to you. Only traits controlled by genes can be acted upon by natural selection. Genetic variations contribute to the diversity of organisms.

Inherited Traits

Figure 6 Variations in traits depend on the traits that parents pass on to their offspring.

1. **Make Observations** List several inherited variations you can observe in this group of students.

....
....
....
....
....
....
....
....
....
....

2. **CCC Cause and Effect** How did the students in **Figure 6** get such variations in traits?

....
....

Figure 7 A mutation caused the flower on the right to grow in an unusual way.

Explain Phenomena Describe how the mutation changed the flower.

....

....

....

....

Mutations Sexual reproduction causes existing gene variations to be recombined in each member of a population. To get a new variation, there must be a gene mutation. A mutation is any change to the genetic material. **Figure 7** shows a flower with an obvious mutation. Only mutations to sex chromosomes can be passed on to offspring. In humans, new genetic variations are introduced by mutations to egg or sperm cells. A mutation to a body cell, such as a heart or brain cell, only affects the individual and is not passed on to offspring. If offspring are born with a mutation, natural selection will determine whether that mutation gets passed on to the next generation.

Epigenetic Changes Epigenetics is the study of small changes to DNA that turn genes on or off but do not change the genetic code itself. All the cells in your body have identical DNA, but functions vary greatly. Gene expression determines how a cell acts—whether it will function as a bone cell or a skin cell. In your lifetime, there will be small chemical changes to your DNA affecting how genes get expressed. Your offspring can inherit these changes.

Inherited changes can affect multiple generations. For example, smoking makes small changes to DNA. Due to epigenetics, a grandmother who smokes is more likely to have a grandchild with asthma. The grandchild will inherit the same epigenetic changes that smoking caused in his or her grandmother. Epigenetics is challenging the idea that natural selection acts on genetic variation alone. Scientists are working to understand how a gene that gets turned on or off in a body cell could show up two generations later.

 INTERACTIVITY

Explore how a lack of genetic variations can impact crops.

 VIDEO

Watch a video about natural selection.

✓ CHECK POINT **Distinguish Facts** A mutation can be inherited only if it occurs in which type of cell?

MS-LS4-4, MS-LS4-5, MS-LS4-6

1. **Identify** Darwin identified three factors affecting the process of natural selection. What are they?

....

2. **Determine Differences** The terms *mechanism* and *natural selection* both refer to natural processes. What makes them different?

....
....
....
....

3. **Evaluate Claims** A classmate claims that all mutations are harmful and can be passed on. Is this true? Explain.

....
....
....
....
....

4. **Apply Scientific Reasoning** How does natural selection help a species to evolve?

....
....
....

5. **SEP Construct Explanations** How does the genetic variation of traits within a population affect its probability for survival? Explain.

....
....
....
....
....
....

6. **CCC Cause and Effect** Sea turtles can lay 50 to 200 eggs in a nest. Some eggs get destroyed or eaten by other animals. The young turtles that hatch face many challenges as they head to the ocean. They may have to crawl over steep slopes, through seaweed, or around obstacles. Raccoons, foxes, crabs, birds, fish, and sharks may eat them. Given the challenges and the data in the Math Toolbox, write an expression and use it to calculate the percent hatched. Use the percent to roughly estimate the number of sea turtles from a nest of 100 in Naples that reach the ocean safely. Express your answer as a percentage.

....
....
....
....
....
....
....

7. **SEP Develop Models** ✏ Draw a young turtle and the variations you think could make it more successful. Label the variations and explain how they would benefit the turtle.

MS-LS4-4, MS-LS4-5, MS-LS4-6

Fossils from Bedrock

▶ VIDEO

Explore the techniques and technologies that scientists use to extract fossils.

Do you know how to get a fossil out of a rock? You engineer it! Scientists use several methods to extract these remains of the past.

The Challenge: To remove fossils from bedrock without damaging them or the surrounding area.

Phenomenon Fossils stay trapped under layers of rock for millions of years. When the geology of an area changes, these layers are sometimes exposed. This offers a great opportunity to search for evidence of how adaptation by natural selection contributes to the evolution of a species.

Removing a fragile fossil from rock takes skill, time, and special tools. Sometimes fossil collectors have to dig out the larger section of rock holding a fossil. Until recently, extracting a fossil meant slowly and carefully chipping away at the rock with a small chisel and hammer, then sweeping away rock dust with a small brush. The latest technology is the pneumatic drill pen. Vibrating at 30,000 times each minute, the drill pen carves out a fossil more quickly and with greater control. Another method is the acid wash. While it takes much longer than the mechanical methods, and can only be used on fossils found in limestone and chalk, an acid wash is the safest way to remove an undamaged fossil.

Scientists carefully brush away dirt and debris from bones discovered in dig sites to gather fossil evidence of how organisms have changed over time.

DESIGN CHALLENGE

How would you modify the process for removing fossils from bedrock? Go to the Engineering Design Notebook to find out!

HANDS-ON LAB

uInvestigate Explore how different birds' feet help them survive in their environments.

MS-LS3-1 Develop and use a model to describe why structural changes to genes (mutations) located on chromosomes may affect proteins and may result in harmful, beneficial, or neutral effects to the structure and function of the organism.

MS-LS4-4 Construct an explanation based on evidence that describes how genetic variations of traits in a population increase some individuals' probability of surviving and reproducing in a specific environment.

MS-LS4-6 Use mathematical representations to support explanations of how natural selection may lead to increases and decreases of specific traits in populations over time.

Connect It!

✎ **Label each duck as either male or female.**

SEP Construct Explanations Do you think that both ducks' appearance could be a result of natural selection? Explain your reasoning.

....

....

....

Processes of Evolution

Charles Darwin's theory of natural selection is straightforward. Any population of living things has inherited variations. In addition, the population produces more young than can survive. According to natural selection, only the individuals that are well-adapted to their environments will survive and reproduce. An organism's **fitness** describes how well it can survive and reproduce in its environment. According to Darwin's theory, the fittest individuals survive to reproduce and pass their traits to the next generation. Organisms with low fitness are not as well-adapted to their environment and may die without reproducing or may not have as many offspring. Over time, as individual organisms successfully respond to changing conditions in the environment, the population evolves and its fitness increases.

Beyond Natural Selection Observe the male and female mandarin ducks in **Figure 1**. Both ducks have many adaptations that help them survive and reproduce in their watery habitat. Oily feathers keep the ducks dry. Webbed feet propel the ducks quickly through the water. Nesting in trees keeps ducklings safe from predators. Dull colors help the female duck blend in with her background. Now, look at the male duck. He seems to be calling for attention! His brightly colored face and the bold black and white stripes on his sides surely attract predators. How could natural selection result in traits that hurt the male duck's chance of survival? Answer: There is more to evolution than "survival of the fittest."

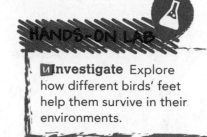

HANDS-ON LAB

Investigate Explore how different birds' feet help them survive in their environments.

▶ VIDEO

Learn about the process of evolution.

Opposites Attract
Figure 1 Believe it or not, these ducks are both from the same species. Male and female mandarin ducks have evolved to look very different!

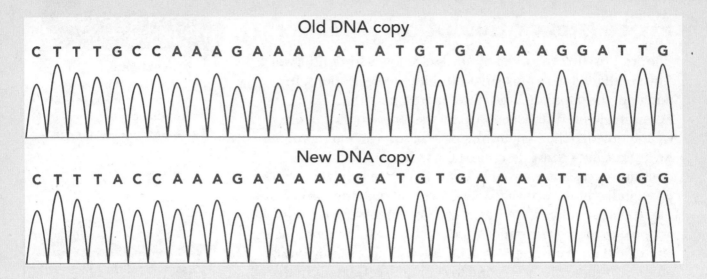

Old DNA copy

C T T T G C C A A A G A A A A A T A T G T G A A A A G G A T T G

New DNA copy

C T T T A C C A A A G A A A A A G A T G T G A A A A T T A G G G

Spellcheck, Please!

Figure 2 🖉 A mutation is like a spelling error in a gene's DNA sequence. Any change in the sequence results in a mutation. Observe how the sequence changes. Compare the sequences of the two DNA copies. Circle any differences you observe in the new DNA copy.

Explain Phenomena What do you think may have caused the differences between the two DNA copies?

....

....

 **INTERACTIVITY**

Analyze mutations and how they can impact evolution.

Mutations One reason for Darwin's oversimplification of evolution was that he did not yet know about mutations. You've already learned that a mutation is any change to an organism's genetic material. Mutations can create multiple alleles, or forms of a gene. Different alleles cause variations in traits such as eye color, ear shape, and blood type.

How Mutations Happen Mutations are created in two ways. First, a dividing cell can make an error while copying its DNA (**Figure 2**). There are approximately six billion units in one copy of human DNA. Imagine copying by hand a book that had six billion letters. Think how easy it would be to make a mistake! Researchers estimate that each human child inherits an average of 60 new mutations from his or her parents. That sounds like a lot, doesn't it? But it means that the body makes only one mistake out of every 100 million units of DNA copied. Secondly, mutations also occur when an organism is exposed to environmental factors such as radiation or certain chemicals that damage the cell's DNA. While the cell has mechanisms to repair damaged DNA, that repair is not always perfect. Any mistake while fixing the DNA results in a mutation.

Effects of Mutations Most mutations are neutral—they have no effect on the individual's function. The mutation may be in a part of the DNA that is inactive. Out of the mutations that do affect function, most are harmful to the individual. Randomly changing a process in the body typically results in decreased function. Only mutations on sex chromosomes can get passed on and affect the fitness of offspring. A beneficial mutation that increases fitness tends to grow more common in a population. A mutation that decreases fitness tends to disappear because the individuals with that mutation die or reproduce less successfully.

Need for Mutations People often think of mutations as harmful. It's true that mutations can lead to cancer and genetic defects. At the same time, however, mutations are necessary for evolution to occur. Mutations create all the variations among members of a species and account for the diversity of organisms on Earth. **Figure 3** shows how mutations can change plant leaf shapes. Imagine if the first single-celled organisms had never experienced mutation! That first species would have been the only life that ever existed on the planet.

☑ CHECK POINT **Summarize Text** How are mutations both harmful and beneficial?

....

....

Academic Vocabulary

List where you may have heard the word *random* used before. What does *randomly* mean as it's used here?

....

....

....

....

✋ **INTERACTIVITY**

Explore what might happen when a population of squirrels is separated by landforms.

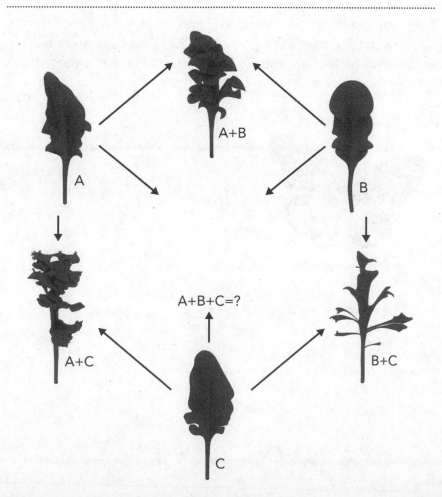

Variations from Mutations

Figure 3 Scientists studied how three mutations in mustard plant DNA (labeled A, B, and C in the image) affect leaf shape.

SEP Use a Model to Predict 🖉 Examine the effects of the mutations on leaf shape. In the center of the image, draw what you think the leaves would look like if a plant had all three mutations.

Coevolution and Cooperation

Figure 4 The acacia tree and ants both evolved features that help them work together.

Infer What features do you think the acacia tree and the ants might have that would help one another?

....

....

....

....

....

If you break down the word *interactions*, it means "the actions between." How would you define interactions between two species?

....

....

....

....

Coevolution

Two or more species with close interactions can affect each other's evolution. Coevolution is the process by which two species evolve in response to changes in each other over time. Coevolution can happen when species cooperate with each other, as shown in **Figure 4**. Several acacia trees in Central America have coevolved with select species of ants. The acacia trees evolved hollow thorns and nectar pores because of their close interactions with the ants. Likewise, the ants evolved defense behaviors to protect "their" trees. A queen ant lays her eggs in the hollow thorns of an acacia tree. In return for the shelter and food from the tree, the ants protect the tree. They attack when other insects or animals try to devour the acacia leaves. Other examples of interactions that can lead to coevolution include species that compete for resources and species that may be prey to a predator.

Model It!

Mimicry in Coevolution

Figure 5 Tiger-wing butterflies evolved to absorb and store toxins from plants they ate when they were caterpillars. This makes them taste bad. Birds avoid eating tiger-wing butterflies and other butterflies that mimic, or closely resemble, them.

SEP Develop Models ✏ Sketch the progression of how a butterfly's wing patterns may have changed over time to mimic that of the tiger-wing butterfly.

☑LESSON 3 Check

MS-LS3-1, MS-LS4-4, MS-LS4-6

1. SEP Communicate Information What does fitness mean in terms of evolution?

....
....
....
....

2. Apply Scientific Reasoning What are the two ways in which mutations can occur? Give at least one example of an environmental factor.

....
....
....
....
....
....

3. SEP Construct Explanations Explain the role of mutations in genetic variation and in the diversity of living things. Support your explanation with evidence.

....
....
....
....
....
....
....
....
....
....

4. Distinguish Relationships Consider two species that compete for the same resources. Could their interactions affect each other's evolution? Explain.

....
....
....
....
....
....

Quest CHECK-IN

In this lesson, you learned how a population can be influenced by natural selection, species interactions, and genetic variations due to mutations.

CCC Cause and Effect Why is it important to consider the role of genetic variations when trying to determine what caused the changes to the European blackcaps?

....
....
....
....

INTERACTIVITY

Evolution of the Blackcaps

Go online to investigate factors that may have caused the variations in the European blackcaps.

Evidence in the Fossil Record

uInvestigate Model how different fossils form.

MS-LS4-1 Analyze and interpret data for patterns in the fossil record that document the existence, diversity, extinction, and change of life forms throughout the history of life on Earth under the assumption that natural laws operate today as in the past.

MS-LS4-2 Apply scientific ideas to construct an explanation for the anatomical similarities and differences among modern organisms and between modern and fossil organisms to infer evolutionary relationships.

MS-LS4-3 Analyze displays of pictorial data to compare patterns of similarities in the embryological development across multiple species to identify relationships not evident in the fully formed anatomy.

MS-LS4-6 Use mathematical representations to support explanations of how natural selection may lead to increases and decreases of specific traits in populations over time. (Also **EP&CIIa and EP&CIIc**)

Connect It !

✎ **Draw arrows to connect similar features between the fossil and the modern animal.**

Interpret Photos Which parts of the crinoid's tentacles are best preserved in the fossils? Which parts were not preserved?

....

....

....

The Fossil Record

Fossils are preserved remains or traces of living things. **Figure 1** shows fossils of crinoids, relatives of modern-day starfish. All the fossils that have been discovered and what we have learned from them make up the fossil record. It is called a record because the fossils form data patterns that scientists can understand through measurement and observation. The fossil record documents the diversity of the life forms, many now extinct, and shows how life forms existed and changed throughout Earth's history. The fossil record is a treasure trove of evidence about how organisms of the past evolved into the forms we see today.

Microevolution and Macroevolution
Scientists can observe evolution taking place within populations of organisms. Small, gradual changes in the color or size of a certain population is called microevolution. *Micro-* means very small, and *evolution* means change through time. One example of microevolution is the northern population of house sparrows. They adapted to a colder climate by growing larger bodies than the southern population. This small change took less than 100 years. Usually, for multicellular organisms, it takes years to thousands of years for a new species to develop. Scientists turn to the fossil record to learn about macroevolution, or major evolutionary change.

A Glimpse of the Past
Figure 1 Crinoids are relatives of starfish. We can learn a lot about the evolution of crinoids by looking at fossils of their extinct relatives. Some ancient crinoids grew more than 40 meters long!

1. **An organism dies and sinks to the bottom of a lake.**

2.

Forming a Fossil

Figure 2 A fossil may form when sediment quickly covers a dead organism.

Relate Text to Visuals
🖊 The images and captions are shown in the correct order. Fill in the missing caption for image 2.

Many Kinds of Fossils

Figure 3 A fossil may be the preserved remains of an organism's body, or the trace of an organism—something it leaves behind.

1. **Classify** 🖊 Label each image as either a body fossil or a trace fossil.

2. **SEP Evaluate Evidence** Why did you classify them that way?

....
....
....
....
....

How Fossils Form

How Fossils Form A fossil is the impression that an organism or part of an organism leaves in rock. That impression comes about in one of two ways. A mold creates a hollow area in the rock that is the shape of an organism or part of an organism. Or, a cast makes a solid copy of an organism's shape, sometimes containing some of the original organism.

Most fossils form when living things die and sediment buries them. Sediment is the small, solid pieces of material that come from rocks or the remains of organisms and settle to the bottom of a body of water. Over time, the sediment slowly hardens into rock and preserves the shapes of the organisms. Fossils can form from any kind of living thing, from bacteria to dinosaurs.

Many fossils come from organisms that once lived in or near still water. Swamps, lakes, and shallow seas build up sediment quickly and bury remains of living things. In **Figure 2**, you can see how a fossil might form. When an organism dies, its soft parts usually decay quickly or are eaten by other organisms. Only hard parts of an organism typically leave fossils. These hard parts include bones, shells, teeth, seeds, and woody stems. It is rare for the soft parts of an organism to become a fossil. People often see fossils after erosion exposes them. Erosion is the wearing away of Earth's surface by natural processes such as water and wind.

Snail shells

Turtle dropping

3. Over millions of years, the sediment hardens into rock, preserving the remains.

4. As rock erodes, the fossil is exposed on the surface.

Kinds of Fossils

There are two types of fossils: body fossils and trace fossils. Each one gives us different information about the ancient organism it represents.

HANDS-ON LAB

Investigate Model how different fossils form.

Body Fossils Body fossils preserve the shape and structure of an organism. We can learn about what a plant or animal looked like from a body fossil. Body fossils of trees are called petrified wood. The term *petrified* means "turned into stone." Petrified fossils are fossils in which minerals replace all or part of an organism. In petrified wood, the remains are so well preserved that scientists can often count the rings to tell how old a tree was when it died millions of years ago. Ancient mammoths frozen into ice, petrified dinosaur bones, and insects trapped in amber are other examples of body fossils.

Trace Fossils We can learn what an animal did from trace fossils. Footprints, nests, and animal droppings preserved in stone are all trace fossils, as shown in **Figure 3**.

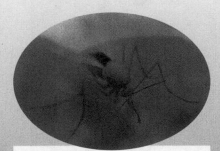

Mosquito in amber

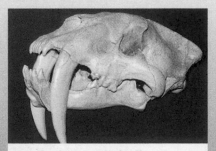

Smilodon, cat skull

Dinosaur tracks

Fossil Evidence of Evolution

Most of what we know about ancient organisms comes from the fossil record. The fossil record provides evidence about the history of life and past environments on Earth. The fossil record also shows how different groups of organisms have changed over time. Each new discovery helps to fill holes in our understanding of evolution.

Early Earth When Earth first formed, more than 4.5 billion years ago, it was extremely hot. Earth was likely mostly melted. As Earth cooled, solid rocks became stable at Earth's surface. The oldest known fossils are from rocks that formed about a billion years after Earth formed. **Figure 4** shows a rock made of these fossils. Scientists think that all other forms of life on Earth arose from these simple organisms.

Scientists cannot yet pinpoint when or where life first evolved. Scientists hypothesize that life first evolved in Earth's ocean. The early ocean contained reactive chemicals. Under the right conditions, sunlight and lightning can change those chemicals into molecules similar to those found in living cells. More research will help scientists to settle the question of the origin of life on Earth.

Fossils Reveal Early Life

Figure 4 Stromatolites are rock-like structures formed by layers of fossilized bacteria. Dating as far back as 3.4 billion years ago, they are the oldest evidence of life forms on Earth. Ancient bacteria in water produced thin sheets of film that trapped mud. Over time, these thin sheets formed microfossils—fossils too small to see without a microscope. Eventually, the sheets built up into the layers you see here.

Interpret Photos Using evidence in the picture, determine the oldest and youngest layers. Then, draw a vertical scale next to the stromatolite to show which are the oldest layers and which are the youngest.

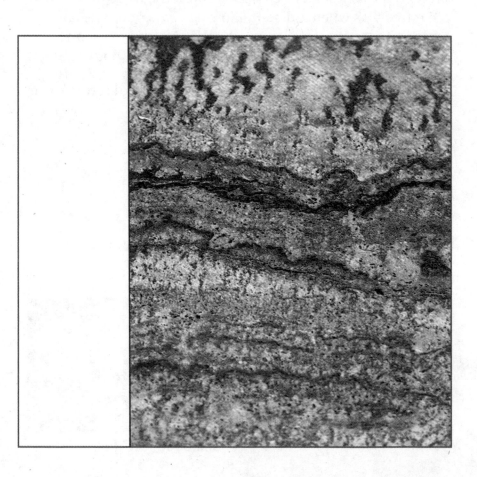

Gomphotherium
24–5 mya

Moeritherium
36 mya

Platybelodon
'23–5.3 mya

Mammut americanum
(American mastodon)
4 mya–11,500 ya

Mammuthus
(Woolly Mammoth)
Pliocene, from
750,000–11,500 ya

Loxodonta
(African elephant)
1.8 mya–present

ya = years ago; mya = millions of years ago

Fossils and Evolution Through Time

The fossil record provides evidence that life on Earth has evolved. Rock forms in layers, with newer layers on top of older layers. When we dig deeper, we see older rocks with fossils from earlier time periods. The oldest rocks contain fossils of only very simple organisms. Younger rocks include fossils of both simple organisms and also more complex organisms. Scientists also place fossils in chronological order using radioactive dating, which uses radioactive isotopes of elements to assign an age range to a fossil. Looking at fossils in rocks from different time periods, scientists can reconstruct the history of evolution. **Figure 5** shows the evolution of the elephant, reconstructed from the fossil record.

The fossil record also shows how Earth's climate has changed. Some plant fossils reveal surprises, such as palm trees in Wyoming and giant tropical ferns in Antarctica. Fossils and preserved remains are also evidence of how climate change influences evolution.

Evolution of the Modern Elephant

Figure 5 Scientists have reconstructed the evolutionary history of the elephant with evidence from the fossil record.

☑ CHECK POINT **Cite Textual Evidence** Would you expect to find fossils related to the evolution of the elephant in the oldest rocks in the fossil record? Explain.

....
....
....
....

Question It !

Kyle has very limited vision and needs someone to explain the evolution of elephants to him. Suppose you are going to work with Kyle to help him understand the changes elephants have undergone.

Interpret Diagrams Using **Figure 5**, what features of the animals have stayed the same? What features have changed?

....
....
....
....
....

INTERACTIVITY

Analyze and compare the structure and development of embryos to determine evolutionary relationships.

Comparisons of Anatomy

The structure of an organism's body is called its anatomy. Similarities in anatomy between organisms from the fossil record and organisms living today are clues they evolved from a common ancestor. These clues include similarities in embryological development. They help us to reconstruct evolutionary history.

Embryological Development

An embryo is a young organism that develops from a fertilized egg (called a zygote). The growing embryo may develop inside or outside the parent's body. The early development of different organisms in an embryo shows some striking similarities that are not present in the fully developed organisms. For example, chickens, fish, turtles, and pigs all resemble each other during the early stages of development. Anatomical similarities in early development suggest that organisms are related and share a common ancestor.

Scientists can also analyze fossilized eggs to infer lines of descent. **Figure 6** shows the model of a duck-billed dinosaur embryo, known as a hadrosaur, compared to an x-ray of a chicken embryo. You can see many anatomical similarities in their early development.

Homologous Structures

Similar structures that related species have inherited from a common ancestor are known as homologous structures (hoh MAHL uh gus). Bats, dogs, dolphins, and even flying reptiles have homologous structures in their limbs. Although the structures look very different now, the Math Toolbox shows you the bones that these animals all have in common.

INTERACTIVITY

Examine patterns of anatomical similarities and differences among organisms.

Birds and Dinosaurs

Figure 6 ✏ Draw lines and label the features that look similar in both the hadrosaur and chicken embryos.

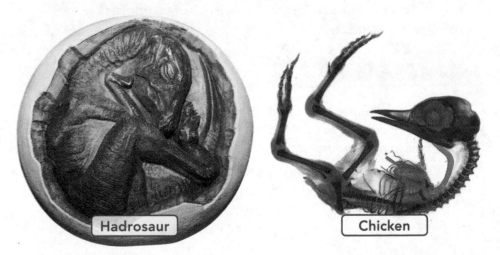

Hadrosaur

Chicken

Homologous Anatomical Structures

The wings, flipper, and leg of these organisms all have similar anatomical (body) structures. Note that the structures are not drawn to scale.

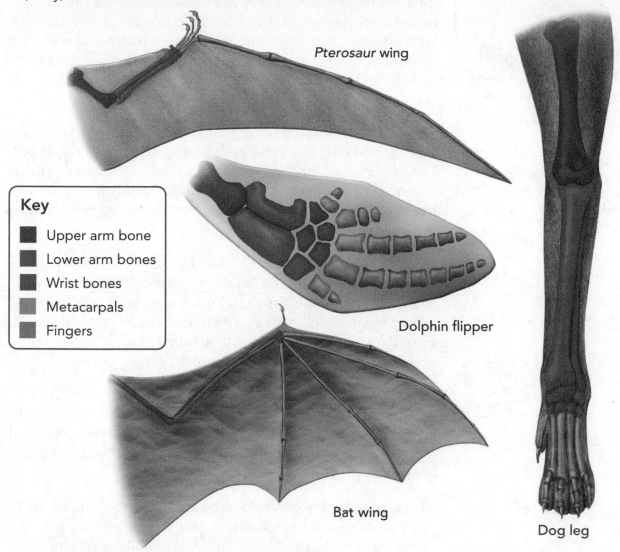

Pterosaur wing

Key

- ■ Upper arm bone
- ■ Lower arm bones
- ■ Wrist bones
- ■ Metacarpals
- ■ Fingers

Dolphin flipper

Bat wing

Dog leg

1. **Construct Tables** ✎ Choose two of the animals shown above to examine closely. Using a metric ruler, measure the upper arm bone, the lower arm bone, and the fingers. Create a data table to the right and record the measurements in millimeters.

2. **CCC Analyze Proportional Relationships** In each species, compare the upper arm to lower arm, or compare fingers to metacarpals. Can you find any equivalent ratios?

....

....

....

....

INTERACTIVITY

Interpret data from the fossil record that supports species extinction.

VIDEO

Find evidence for evolution in the fossil record.

Beginning and End of a Species

Natural selection explains how variations can lead to changes in a species. A new species forms when one population remains isolated from the rest of its species long enough to evolve such different traits that members of the isolated population can no longer mate and produce offspring capable of reproduction with members of any other populations of the species. **Figure 7** shows an example of a turtle species that has evolved seven different subspecies. Over time, the subspecies could form separate species.

Gradual Change Some species in the fossil record seem to change gradually over time, such as the elephants in **Figure 5**. The time scale of the fossil record involves thousands or millions of years. There is plenty of time for gradual changes to produce new species. The fossil record contains many examples of species that are halfway between two others.

Rapid Change At times, new, related species suddenly appear in the fossil record. Rapid evolution can follow a major change in environmental conditions. A cooling climate, for example, can put a lot of stress on a population. Only the individuals adapted to cooler conditions will survive. Through natural selection, the population may rapidly evolve to a new species.

Extinction A species is extinct if it no longer exists and will never again live on Earth. A rapid environmental change is more likely to cause extinction than a new species. The fossil record shows that most of the species that ever lived on Earth are now extinct.

New predators, climate change, disease, and competition with other species are a few factors that can lead to extinction. According to natural selection, if a species fails to develop the adaptations necessary to survive the changing conditions in an environment, that species will not survive and reproduce. Small populations that breed slowly and cannot relocate are more likely to become extinct. The fossil record shows that volcanic eruptions, asteroids striking Earth, and sudden climate change can kill off many species in a short time.

✓ CHECK POINT **Translate Information** How do you know that the animals whose limbs are depicted in the Math Toolbox had a common ancestor at one point? What question could you ask to find out more and why would you ask it?

....

....

....

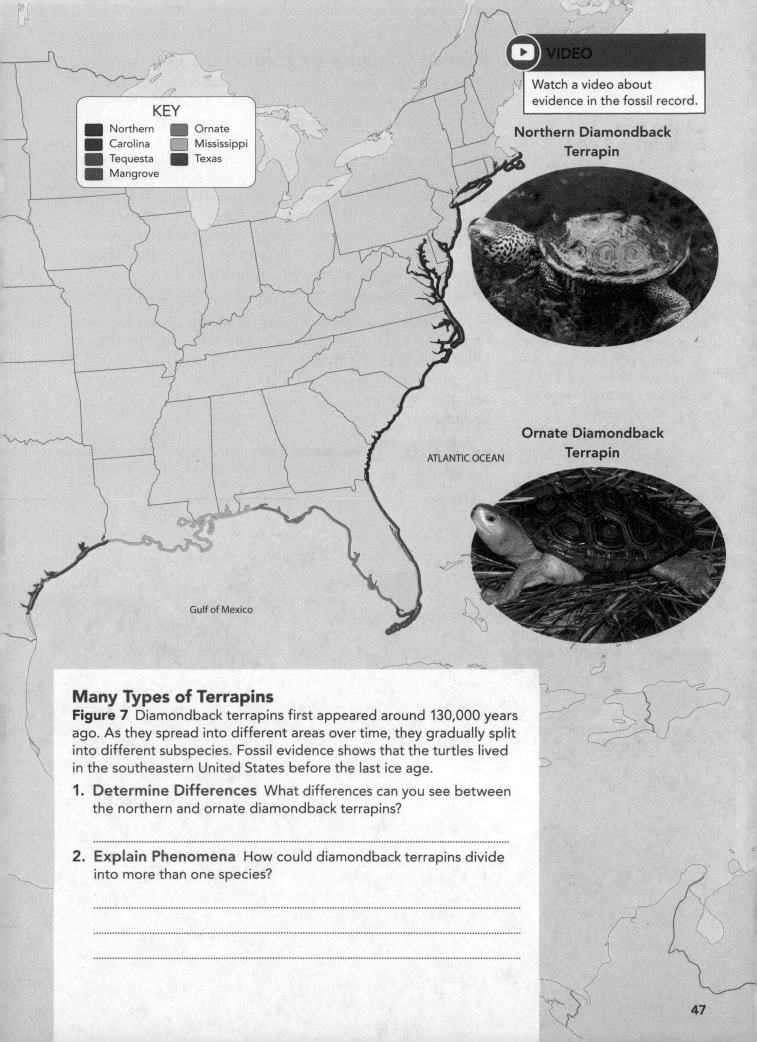

KEY

- Northern
- Carolina
- Tequesta
- Mangrove
- Ornate
- Mississippi
- Texas

Northern Diamondback Terrapin

ATLANTIC OCEAN

Gulf of Mexico

Ornate Diamondback Terrapin

Many Types of Terrapins

Figure 7 Diamondback terrapins first appeared around 130,000 years ago. As they spread into different areas over time, they gradually split into different subspecies. Fossil evidence shows that the turtles lived in the southeastern United States before the last ice age.

1. **Determine Differences** What differences can you see between the northern and ornate diamondback terrapins?

   ....

2. **Explain Phenomena** How could diamondback terrapins divide into more than one species?

   ....

   ....

   ....

California's Endangered Whales

Figure 8 California has six species of whales on the endangered species list: the north Pacific right, blue, sei, fin, humpback, and the sperm whale.

SEP Cite Textual Evidence

Some species of whale have struggled to overcome over-hunting by humans that occurred more than 100 years ago. Why might it be so difficult for these large mammals to recover?

....

....

....

....

Human Influence on Extinction

Some extinctions are the direct result of human activities. Species cannot survive over-hunting, sudden climate change, and indirect changes to their habitat caused by the actions of human communities. The six species of endangered whales on North America's Pacific coast have suffered from these kinds of changes. As they move within their habitat, some whales are hunted, injured by ships, and are injured in fishing gear. Though whale hunting has been banned since 1949, the northern Pacific right whale population is not recovering. The recovery plan includes reducing injuries from fishing gear, reducing ship collisions, protecting habitats, and continuing the hunting ban. **Figure 8** shows three endangered species of whales living in the waters off California.

Many scientists think extinctions are rapidly increasing. Organisms like whales, who reproduce slowly and produce fewer variations over time, cannot adapt quickly through natural selection to recover from sudden, extreme human activities. We may lose the largest animals ever to live on Earth.

☑ **CHECK POINT** **Summarize Text** How might humans influence the extinction of a species, such as whales?

....

....

humpback whale

sperm whale

blue whale

☑ LESSON 4 Check

MS-LS4-1, MS-LS4-2, MS-LS4-3, MS-LS4-6, EP&CIIa

1. **Infer** Refer to the figure **Birds and Dinosaurs**. If two organisms have homologous structures and similar early development, what can you infer about them?

....

....

2. **SEP Analyze Data**
According to the fossil record, which level in the rock layers shown in the diagram will have the oldest organisms? Explain.

....

....

....

....

....

....

3. **SEP Construct Explanations** How do you account for differences between the bat's wing and the dolphin's flipper?

....

....

....

....

Dolphin flipper

Bat wing

4. **SEP Engage in Argument** What can you say to back the claim that the fossil record supports the theory of evolution?

....

....

....

....

5. **CCC Describe Patterns** If you were a scientist trying to determine if an organism evolved gradually or rapidly, how would patterns in the fossil record help you? Explain how the pattern would provide evidence to support the rate of evolution for that organism.

....

....

....

....

....

....

....

....

....

....

6. **Apply Scientific Reasoning** Why is a sudden change in the environment more likely to cause a species to go extinct rather than to cause a new species to develop?

....

....

....

....

....

....

Other Evidence of Evolution

HANDS-ON LAB

uInvestigate
Explore how DNA provides evidence for evolution.

MS-LS4-2 Apply scientific ideas to construct an explanation for the anatomical similarities and differences among modern organisms and between modern and fossil organisms to infer evolutionary relationships.

MS-LS4-6 Use mathematical representations to support explanations of how natural selection may lead to increases and decreases of specific traits in populations over time.

Connect It!

🖉 **Count the number of different kinds of organisms you see and write your number in the white circle on the photograph.**

SEP Evaluate Evidence What do all the organisms in the photo have in common, and what does this suggest about how closely related they are to one another?

....

....

....

Using Technology to Study Evolution

Advances in technology have led to new knowledge about evolution. Darwin and scientists of his time used their eyes, hand tools, and simple microscopes to study evolution. Darwin's microscope had less than 200x magnification. Modern scientists have much better tools. We now have such powerful microscopes and imaging devices that computers can show us the shapes of individual molecules. Future advances may further our understanding of evolution.

Genetic Material and Evolution The coral reef in **Figure 1** contains an amazing variety of living things. The diverse shapes, body structures, and lifestyles are all due to differences in genetic material, the set of chemical instructions that guide the function and growth of an organism. Evolution results from changes in genetic material. Small changes in genetic material lead to microevolution within species. An accumulation of small changes causes macroevolution, or the creation of new species.

INTERACTIVITY

Discuss how a device or object you use every day has changed over time.

Literacy Connection

Read and Comprehend As you work your way through this lesson, stop frequently to see if you understand what you just read. Each paragraph has key information. Try to restate it in your own words.

Rainbow of Life on a Reef
Figure 1 All of the differences among the organisms in this coral reef at Anacapa Island, California result from evolutionary changes in genetic material.

Genetic Evidence for a Common Ancestor

Every living thing uses DNA for genetic material. Mosquitoes, humans, plants, and bacteria all have cells with the same system of genetic material. The shared use of DNA is one piece of evidence that every organism on Earth has a common ancestor. This common ancestor, called LUCA for Last Universal Common Ancestor, was most likely a single-celled organism similar to modern bacteria or archaea.

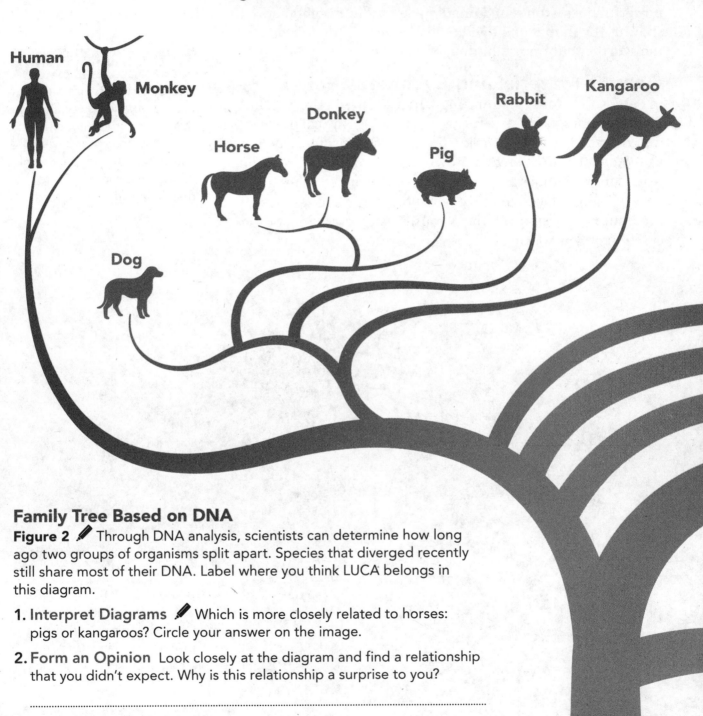

Family Tree Based on DNA

Figure 2 ✎ Through DNA analysis, scientists can determine how long ago two groups of organisms split apart. Species that diverged recently still share most of their DNA. Label where you think LUCA belongs in this diagram.

1. **Interpret Diagrams** ✎ Which is more closely related to horses: pigs or kangaroos? Circle your answer on the image.

2. **Form an Opinion** Look closely at the diagram and find a relationship that you didn't expect. Why is this relationship a surprise to you?

....

....

....

Dawn of Evolution DNA is a complex molecule, difficult to copy without making any mistakes. LUCA started to change as it accumulated mutations, or changes to its DNA. Natural selection and other processes shaped LUCA's evolution. The original population of LUCA split and diverged, evolving into all the species that live or have ever lived on Earth. The traces of this evolution are recorded in the DNA of every organism. Shared DNA between species provides evidence of the evolutionary past. The more similar the DNA between two species, the more closely related they are. **Figure 2** shows a family tree based on differences in one stretch of DNA.

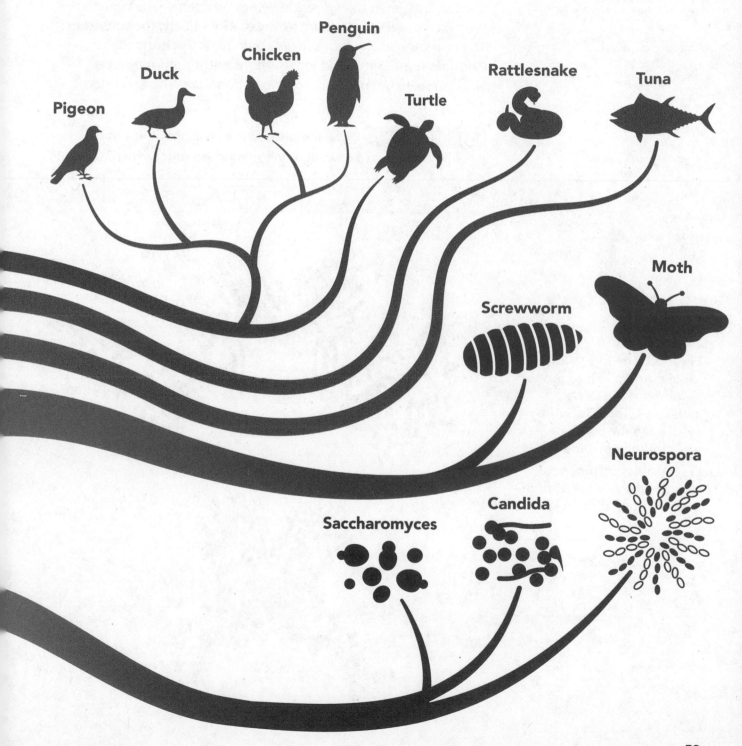

INTERACTIVITY

Explore how different types of evidence help to establish evolutionary relationships.

▶ VIDEO

Learn about a career in evolutionary biology.

Proteins

Recall that genes code for different **proteins**, which are complicated molecules that carry out important cellular functions. Proteins can act as the building blocks for cell materials and carry out important cellular functions. For example, some muscle fibers are made of chains of the protein actin. Other proteins act as messengers, fight diseases, carry out chemical reactions, or carry materials around the body.

Proteins and Evolution Consider what could happen to the function of a protein if the gene for it contains a mutation. The mutant genetic material may code for a different form of the protein, as shown in **Figure 3**. The new version of the protein may increase the individual's fitness. More likely, the mutation will lower the individual's fitness or leave it unchanged. Changes in proteins lead to variations within a population. Natural selection acts on those variations, causing evolution.

☑ **CHECK POINT** **Determine Central Ideas** What are the possible effects of a mutation on the function of a protein?

....

....

Mutations and Proteins

Figure 3 The Mre11-Rad50 protein group helps cells to repair breaks in DNA molecules. There is only a small mutation in the genetic code for the bottom form.

Determine Differences How are the two forms of the protein group different?

....

....

....

....

....

....

....

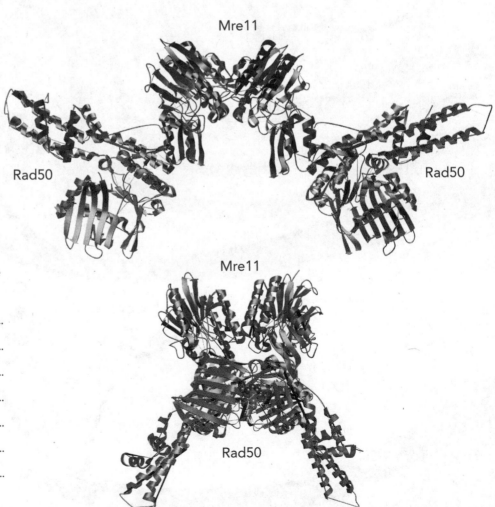

Mre11

Rad50   Rad50

Mre11

Rad50

Protein Analysis and Evolution Scientists compare proteins to see how closely two species are related. In most cases, evidence from DNA and protein structure confirms conclusions based on fossils, embryos, and body structure. For example, DNA comparisons show that dogs are more similar to wolves than to coyotes. This confirms an earlier conclusion based on similarities in the structure and development of the three species.

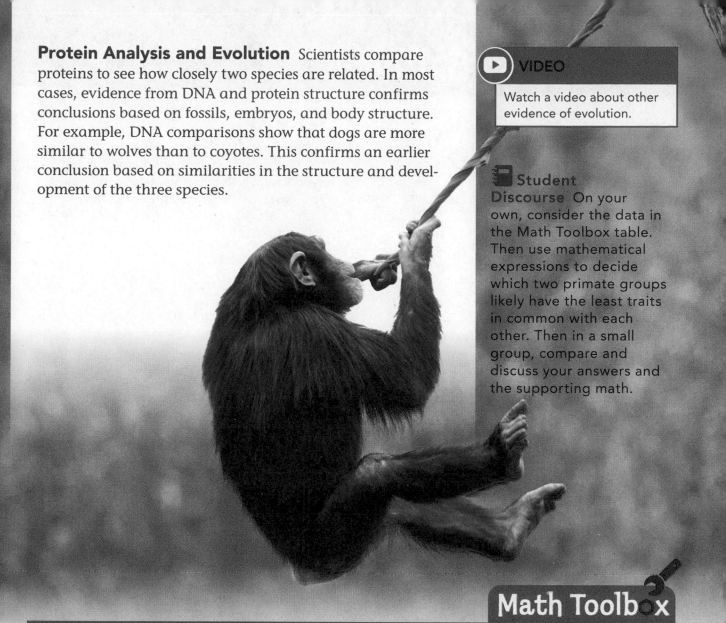

▶ VIDEO

Watch a video about other evidence of evolution.

📓 **Student Discourse** On your own, consider the data in the Math Toolbox table. Then use mathematical expressions to decide which two primate groups likely have the least traits in common with each other. Then in a small group, compare and discuss your answers and the supporting math.

Math Toolbox

All in the Family

Humans, apes, and monkeys are all members of the order Primates. Bonobos, chimpanzees, gorillas, and orangutans are all considered apes, but monkeys are not. Humans and monkeys share about 93 percent of their DNA.

Primate	Genetic Difference with Humans
Bonobo	1.2%
Chimpanzee	1.3%
Gorilla	1.6%
Orangutan	3.1%
Monkey	7.0%

1. **Use Algebraic Expressions** Write an expression representing the percentage of DNA that gorillas share with humans. Let g = gorilla.

....

....

2. **Draw Comparative Inferences** What can you say about the evolutionary relationship between the apes and monkeys compared to humans?

....

....

☑ LESSON 5 Check

1. **SEP Provide Evidence** What evidence is there that every organism on Earth shares a common ancestor?

....

....

2. **Compare and Contrast** What do microevolution and macroevolution have in common? How do they differ?

....

....

....

....

3. **Synthesize Information** How have advances in technology supported the theory of evolution?

....

....

....

....

....

4. **SEP Use Mathematics** Refer to the data table in the Math Toolbox. Given that natural selection acts on variations and influences evolution, which two primate groups would you expect to have the most traits in common? Support your answer with a mathematical expression.

....

....

....

....

5. **Support Your Explanation** What does LUCA stand for and how did it evolve into all the life forms we see today?

....

....

....

....

....

....

....

....

Quest CHECK-IN

In this lesson, you learned more about how genetics drives evolution and how mutations to proteins lead to variations within a population.

CCC Cause and Effect What caused changes to the blackcap populations? How was natural selection at work here?

....

....

....

....

INTERACTIVITY

Prepare Your Report

Go online to investigate the European blackcaps. Look for new information to add to your report. Brainstorm ideas for different ways to represent information.

MS-LS4-2, MS-LS4-4, MS-LS4-5

DNA, Fossils, and Evolution

All living things contain DNA. This blueprint carries the codes for every trait an organism expresses. We now have the technology to extract DNA from living things, as well as fossils, and then map out the locations of all the genes. By comparing modern DNA with that of fossils, it is possible to determine which traits similar species have in common.

Scientists are able to remove and analyze DNA from fossils using a process called an assay. DNA is removed from the center of a fossil and then prepared using an assortment of different chemicals. The DNA sample is then amplified and run through a process called gel electrophoresis. This separates different pieces of the DNA. The results are then compared to known DNA to see how similar they are.

One of the interesting things DNA research has discovered is that the domestication of dogs has changed their diet. While ancestral wolves ate mostly meat, modern dogs have more genes to help them digest starch and other carbohydrates. This suggests that the early dogs who could handle the starches in the human diet had an advantage.

MY DISCOVERY

With a classmate, research how dogs were domesticated from wolves. Engage in a classroom debate about the evidence that supports and refutes the descent of dogs from wolves.

DNA evidence from wolf fossils, like the one shown here, helps to determine the similarities and differences between domestic dogs and their wolf ancestors.

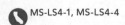

MS-LS4-1, MS-LS4-4

Evidence-Based Assessment

A group of scientists was researching evolutionary relationships. They decided to investigate a particular protein called cytochrome-c. Proteins are made up of compounds called amino acids. They compared the amino acid sequence that codes for the protein among several species. They made a surprising discovery. In moths, whales, and baker's yeast—organisms that do not look at all related—almost half of the positions in the cytochrome-c amino acid sequence were identical.

Cytochrome-c is a very important protein when it comes to releasing energy from food. Like other proteins, cytochrome-c is made of a sequence of amino acids that may or may not vary among organisms. The analysis of cytochrome-c in different organisms provides strong evidence for determining which organisms are closely related. Scientists can predict evolutionary relationships by looking at the amino acid sequences in cytochrome-c that different organisms have in common.

The data table shows ten positions where there are different amino acids in the sequence that codes for the cytochrome-c protein from five different species. In all other positions, the amino acids are the same.

Species	Amino Acid, Position Number in Sequence									
	20	23	52	55	66	68	70	91	97	100
human	M	S	P	S	I	G	D	V	E	A
horse	Q	A	P	S	T	L	E	A	T	E
kangaroo	Q	A	P	T	I	G	D	A	G	A
pig	Q	A	P	S	T	G	E	A	G	E
whale	Q	A	V	S	T	G	E	A	G	A

SOURCE: National Center for Biotechnology Information

Amino Acid Symbols

A = Alanine   M = Methionine

D = Aspartic Acid   P = Proline

E = Glutamic Acid   Q = Glutamine

G = Glycine   S = Serine

I = Isoleucine   T = Threonine

L = Lysine   V = Valine

1. **SEP Analyze Data** According to cytochrome-c analysis, to which other species is the horse most closely related?
   A. human
   B. pig
   C. kangaroo
   D. whale

2. **Support Your Explanation** How did you determine the horse's closest relation among the four species? Use evidence from the data table to support your claim.

....
....
....
....
....
....
....
....
....
....
....
....
....
....

3. **SEP Cite Evidence** Complete the table below to compare the number of different amino acids among the five organisms. Based on the table, circle the organism that is least like the human. Underline the organism that is most like the human.

Organism	Number of Shared Amino Acids with Humans
horse	
kangaroo	
pig	
whale	

4. **SEP Construct Explanations** Cows and sheep have the same sequence of amino acids in their cytochrome-c protein. How is it possible that they can be different species? Select all that apply.

☐ This is the result of convergent evolution.
☐ These two species share a recent common ancestor.
☐ They evolved under different environmental pressures.
☐ They are not closely related.
☐ Similar sequences of cytochrome-c protein do not indicate relatedness.

Quest FINDINGS

Complete the Quest!

Create a multimedia report about the two populations of European blackcaps and what caused them to be so different from each other.

Draw Conclusions If evolution of the blackcaps continues at the current rate, what can be said about similarities of the populations of European blackcaps to their common ancestor and to one another?

....
....
....
....

👆 **INTERACTIVITY**

Reflect on Blackcap Migration

A Bony Puzzle

How can you analyze **patterns** in structures to **show** evolutionary **relationships?**

Background

Phenomenon A new museum of natural history is opening in your community. The director of the museum has asked your class to help with an exhibit about evolutionary history. The director hopes you can show how patterns in skeletons provide clues about common ancestors.

In this investigation, you will analyze and compare the internal and external structures of a pigeon, a bat, and a rabbit. Then you will use the similarities and differences you observe to describe a possible common ancestor and infer evolutionary relationships among these organisms.

Materials

(per group)
- Activity Sheets 1, 2, and 3
- ruler

Rock pigeon
(*Columba livia*)

Eastern cottontail rabbit (*Sylvilagus floridanus*)

Indian flying fox (*Pteropus giganteus*)

Plan Your Investigation

☐ 1. Using the photographs and the diagrams, you will compare the features and structures of the pigeon, bat, and rabbit. You will look for patterns in the skeletons and note similarities and differences among the three animals.

☐ 2. Work with your group to plan a procedure for comparing the skeletons of the three animals. Write out your plan in the space provided. Consider the following questions as a guide for planning your procedure:

* Should we compare all the bones shown in the diagrams or select a few important features that they all have in common to compare?

* Do we also want to include our observations from the photographs of the animals?

* What's the best way to record and organize our observations so we can analyze them more easily? Should we write notes summarizing what we see? Or should we use only data tables to organize the data?

☐ 3. After receiving your teacher's approval, follow the procedure your group developed. Remember that you may need to revise the plan as you carry it out. Record your observations about the three skeletons in the data tables.

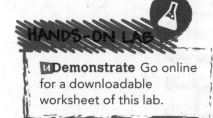

HANDS-ON LAB

ʊDemonstrate Go online for a downloadable worksheet of this lab.

Procedure

Observations

Skeleton	Similarities	Differences
Spine		
Skull		
Limbs		

Photos	Similarities	Differences
covering		
faces		
other		

Analyze and Interpret Data

1. **CCC Identify Patterns** What evidence did you find that will help you describe how these three skeletons are alike?

....

....

....

....

2. **SEP Evaluate Evidence** How does the skeleton pattern that you identified provide evidence for a common ancestor among the pigeon, bat, and rabbit?

....

....

....

3. **Explain Phenomena** Which bones of the common ancestor do you think might have changed the most in its descendants? Which bones remained about the same? Cite evidence from the skeleton diagrams to support your answer.

....

....

....

....

4. **CCC Structure and Function** How are the wings of the bat and the bird, and the rabbit's front legs, all examples of homologous structures? Use evidence from your investigation to support your answer.

....

....

....

5. **SEP Construct Explanations** The museum exhibit will include information to explain evolutionary relationships. What evidence can you use to show that bats share a more recent common ancestor with rabbits than they do with birds?

....

....

....

Could DINOSAURS Roar?

Vegavis is not the direct ancestor of modern-day ducks or chickens, but it is closely related to waterfowl such as geese.

So many movies have dinosaurs roaring as they roam across the landscape shredding trees and devouring prey the size of SUVs. Fossil evidence, however, supports a more silent world. In fact, it wasn't until about 65 to 68 million years ago that a very important piece of anatomy developed—the syrinx. Think of it as a voice box.

In 1992, on an Antarctic island, scientists found a fossil of *Vegavis iaai*, a bird that lived between 68 and 65 million years ago. At that time in Earth's history, Antarctica had a tropical climate. It wasn't until recently that technology revealed the most important find in the fossil: a syrinx.

Connections to Modern-Day Birds

The presence of a syrinx helps us to understand the ancestry of modern birds. Because of the asymmetrical structure of the syrinx, scientists speculate that the bird may have honked like a goose. Scientists analyzed the same structures in 12 living birds and compared them to the next oldest fossilized syrinx that was available. They found similarities in structure across the samples. Their findings supported the claim that *Vegavis iaai* was related to modern birds, but not an ancestor of modern reptiles, who are also able to vocalize through the larynx.

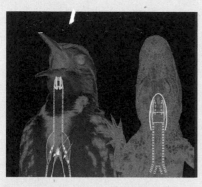

Location of syrinx in living songbird compared to larynx in an alligator

The presence of a syrinx in the *Vegavis iaai* fossil strongly suggests that the bird was capable of producing sounds. In the songbird, as in *Vegavis*, the syrinx is located in the chest. In the alligator, the larynx is located in the throat.

Photo Credit: Dr. Julia Clarke, University of Texas at Austin

It would take a large brain to produce a selection of noises that meant something. If dinosaurs were able to vocalize or utter any sounds at all, then the sounds they made would have been a far cry from what you hear in the movies.

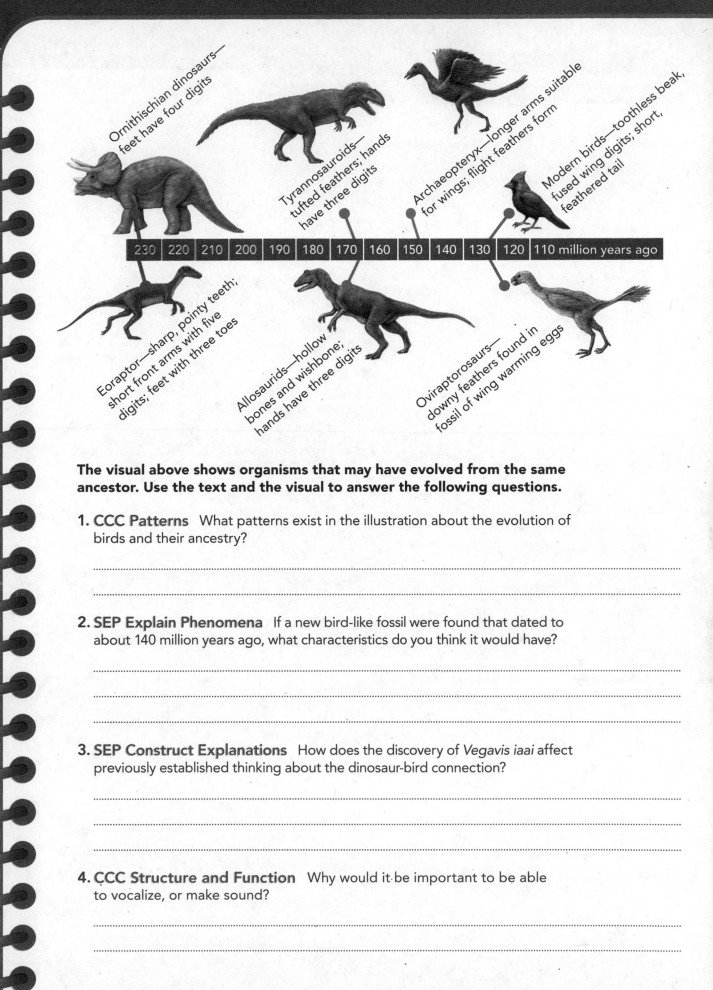

Ornithischian dinosaurs—feet have four digits

Tyrannosauroids—tufted feathers; hands have three digits

Archaeopteryx—longer arms suitable for wings; flight feathers form

Modern birds—toothless beak, fused wing digits; short, feathered tail

| 230 | 220 | 210 | 200 | 190 | 180 | 170 | 160 | 150 | 140 | 130 | 120 | 110 million years ago |

Eoraptor—sharp, pointy teeth; short front arms with five digits; feet with three toes

Allosaurids—hollow bones and wishbone; hands have three digits

Oviraptorosaurs—downy feathers found in fossil of wing warming eggs

The visual above shows organisms that may have evolved from the same ancestor. Use the text and the visual to answer the following questions.

1. **CCC Patterns** What patterns exist in the illustration about the evolution of birds and their ancestry?

....

....

2. **SEP Explain Phenomena** If a new bird-like fossil were found that dated to about 140 million years ago, what characteristics do you think it would have?

....

....

....

3. **SEP Construct Explanations** How does the discovery of *Vegavis iaai* affect previously established thinking about the dinosaur-bird connection?

....

....

....

4. **CCC Structure and Function** Why would it be important to be able to vocalize, or make sound?

....

....

Take Notes

Use this space for recording notes and sketching out ideas.

Evidence Now that you have completed the topic in this segment, do the following task.

Impacts on Evolution in California

Case Study You have learned about the evidence that helps scientists to explain how changes in Earth's system processes and human activities can bring about changes in life forms. Now you can take a closer look at what drives change in a particular species. Consider the impact of climate change due to human activities and how global warming could alter various ecosystems in California. Identify a specific species for your research. It must be a species found in California or along its coasts. The species could be a plant, mammal, bird, reptile, amphibian, or fish. The species may live in California or migrate through it.

Research your chosen species to learn more about it. Find out how long it has inhabited a California ecosystem and if it appears in the fossil record. Determine how your species has changed over time, if at all. Consider what factors might have caused the organism to change. List ways in which your chosen species could adapt to an extreme climate event. What sort of traits would have to be passed from parent to offspring? Also list any steps that could be taken now to protect it from the effects of climate change.

Describe any instance where human activities, either directly or indirectly, might be causing rapid environmental change. Explain how your species could adapt to that change and what might happen if it cannot adapt.

Extreme climate change in California could impact both of these species.

Bull Trout

American Pika

67

Based on your research, answer the following questions.

1. **SEP Communicate Information** Describe the species you researched, its habitat in California, and how climate change is affecting it. Also explain how human activities have directly or indirectly impacted the species.

....

....

....

....

....

....

....

....

....

....

2. **SEP Construct Explanations** If the species you researched goes extinct, how would the species be reflected in the fossil record? Would the species be fossilized? Explain.

....

....

....

....

3. **Explain Phenomena** How could an extreme climate change, such as global warming, affect the evolution of the species you researched? Explain.

....

....

....

....

....

4. **CCC Stability and Change** Natural selection is a process that occurs slowly over time. What sort of adaptations would need to be present in the organism's population in order for it to survive environmental changes, such as the effects of climate change? Can these adaptations be passed from one generation to the next? How does this relate to evolution?

....
....
....
....
....
....
....
....
....

5. **Connect to the Environment** What can humans do to protect your species? Present one way to protect the species with a solution that could be easily implemented.

....
....
....

6. **CCC Cause and Effect** Earlier in this segment, you drew a conclusion about the impact of extreme climate change on leatherback sea turtles in California. Consider what you learned researching your species. How might the human impact of climate change affect the two different species?

....
....
....
....
....
....

Safety Symbols

These symbols warn of possible dangers in the laboratory and remind you to work carefully.

 Safety Goggles Wear safety goggles to protect your eyes in any activity involving chemicals, flames or heating, or glassware.

 Lab Apron Wear a laboratory apron to protect your skin and clothing from damage.

 Breakage Handle breakable materials, such as glassware, with care. Do not touch broken glassware.

 Heat-Resistant Gloves Use an oven mitt or other hand protection when handling hot materials, such as hot plates or hot glassware.

 Plastic Gloves Wear disposable plastic gloves when working with harmful chemicals and organisms. Keep your hands away from your face, and dispose of the gloves according to your teacher's instructions.

 Heating Use a clamp or tongs to pick up hot glassware. Do not touch hot objects with your bare hands.

 Flames Before you work with flames, tie back loose hair and clothing. Follow your teacher's instructions about lighting and extinguishing flames.

 No Flames When using flammable materials, make sure there are no flames, sparks, or other exposed heat sources present.

 Corrosive Chemical Avoid getting acid or other corrosive chemicals on your skin or clothing or in your eyes. Do not inhale the vapors. Wash your hands after the activity.

 Poison Do not let any poisonous chemical come into contact with your skin, and do not inhale its vapors. Wash your hands when you are finished with the activity.

 Fumes Work in a well-ventilated area when harmful vapors may be involved. Avoid inhaling vapors directly. Test an odor only when directed to do so by your teacher, and use a wafting motion to direct the vapor toward your nose.

 Sharp Object Scissors, scalpels, knives, needles, pins, and tacks can cut your skin. Always direct a sharp edge or point away from yourself and others.

 Animal Safety Treat live or preserved animals or animal parts with care to avoid harming the animals or yourself. Wash your hands when you are finished with the activity.

 Plant Safety Handle plants only as directed by your teacher. If you are allergic to certain plants, tell your teacher; do not do an activity involving those plants. Avoid touching harmful plants such as poison ivy. Wash your hands when you are finished with the activity.

 Electric Shock To avoid electric shock, never use electrical equipment around water, when the equipment is wet, or when your hands are wet. Be sure cords are untangled and cannot trip anyone. Unplug equipment not in use.

 Physical Safety When an experiment involves physical activity, avoid injuring yourself or others. Alert your teacher if there is any reason you should not participate.

 Disposal Dispose of chemicals and other laboratory materials safely. Follow the instructions from your teacher.

 Hand Washing Wash your hands thoroughly when finished with an activity. Use soap and warm water. Rinse well.

 General Safety Awareness When this symbol appears, follow the instructions provided. When you are asked to develop your own procedure in a lab, have your teacher approve your plan.

Use this space for recording notes and sketching out ideas.

GLOSSARY

A

abiotic factor A nonliving part of an organism's habitat.

adaptation An inherited behavior or physical characteristic that helps an organism survive and reproduce in its environment.

allele A different form of a gene.

alveoli Tiny sacs of lung tissue specialized for the movement of gases between air and blood.

artery A blood vessel that carries blood away from the heart.

artificial selection The process by which humans breed only those organisms with desired traits to produce the next generation; selective breeding.

asexual reproduction A reproductive process that involves only one parent and produces offspring that are genetically identical to the parent.

autosomal chromosomes The 22 pairs of chromosomes that are not sex chromosomes.

autotroph An organism that is able to capture energy from sunlight or chemicals and use it to produce its own food.

auxin A hormone that controls a plant's growth and response to light.

B

bacteria Single-celled organisms that lack a nucleus; prokaryotes.

behavior The way an organism reacts to changes in its internal conditions or external environment.

biodiversity The number and variety of different species in an area.

biotic factor A living or once living part of an organism's habitat.

brain The part of the central nervous system that is located in the skull and controls most functions in the body.

bronchi The passages that direct air into the lungs.

C

capillary A tiny blood vessel where substances are exchanged between the blood and the body cells.

carbohydrate An energy-rich organic compound, such as a sugar or a starch, that is made of the elements of carbon, hydrogen, and oxygen.

cell The basic unit of structure and function in living things.

cell membrane A thin, flexible barrier that surrounds a cell and controls which substances pass into and out of a cell.

cell wall A rigid supporting layer that surrounds the cells of plants and some other organisms.

cellular respiration The process in which oxygen and glucose undergo a complex series of chemical reactions inside cells, releasing energy.

chlorophyll A green photosynthetic pigment found in the chloroplasts of plants, algae, and some bacteria.

chloroplast An organelle in the cells of plants and some other organisms that captures energy from sunlight and changes it to an energy form that cells can use in making food.

chromosome A threadlike structure within a cell's nucleus that contains DNA that is passed from one generation to the next.

circulatory system An organ system that taransports needed materials to cells and removes wastes.

clone An organism that is genetically identical to the organism from which it was produced.

commensalism A type of symbiosis between two species in which one species benefits and the other species is neither helped nor harmed.

community All the different populations that live together in a certain area.

competition The struggle between organisms to survive as they attempt to use the same limited resources in the same place at the same time.

condensation The change in state from a gas to a liquid.

cones The reproductive structures of gymnosperms.

conservation The practice of using less of a resource so that it can last longer.

consumer An organism that obtains energy by feeding on other organisms.

cytoplasm The thick fluid region of a cell located inside the cell membrane (in prokaryotes) or between the cell membrane and nucleus (in eukaryotes).

D

decomposer An organism that gets energy by breaking down biotic wastes and dead organisms and returns raw materials to the soil and water.

diffusion The process by which molecules move from an area of higher concentration to an area of lower concentration.

digestion The process that breaks complex molecules of food into smaller nutrient molecules.

dominant allele An allele whose trait always shows up in the organism when the allele is present.

dormancy A period of time when an organism's growth or activity stops.

E

ecological restoration The practice of helping a degraded or destroyed ecosystem recover from damage.

ecology The study of how organisms interact with each other and their environment.

ecosystem The community of organisms that live in a particular area, along with their nonliving environment.

ecosystem services The benefits that humans derive from ecosystems.

embryo The young organism that develops from a zygote.

endocytosis The process by which the cell membrane takes particles into the cell by changing shape and engulfing the particles.

energy pyramid A diagram that shows the amount of energy that moves from one feeding level to another in a food web.

enzyme A type of protein that speeds up chemical reactions in the body.

evaporation The process by which molecules at the surface of a liquid absorb enough energy to change to a gas.

evolution Change over time; the process by which modern organisms have descended from ancient organisms.

excretion The process by which wastes are removed from the body.

exocytosis The process by which the vacuole surrounding particles fuses with the cell membrane, forcing the contents out of the cell.

extinct Term used to refer to a group of related organisms that has died out and has no living members.

extinction The disappearance of all members of a species from Earth.

F

fermentation The process by which cells release energy by breaking down food molecules without using oxygen.

fertilization The process in sexual reproduction in which an egg cell and a sperm cell join to form a new cell.

fitness How well an organism can survive and reproduce in its environment.

food chain A series of events in an ecosystem in which organisms transfer energy by eating and by being eaten.

food web The pattern of overlapping feeding relationships or food chains among the various organisms in an ecosystem.

fossil The preserved remains or traces of an organism that lived in the past.

fossil record All the fossils that have been discovered and what scientists have learned from them.

fragmentation A type of asexual reproduction in which a new organism forms from a piece of a parent organism.

fruit The ripened ovary and other structures of an angiosperm that enclose one or more seeds.

G

gene A sequence of DNA that determines a trait and is passed from parent to offspring.

gene therapy The process of replacing an absent or faulty gene with a normal working gene to treat a disease or medical disorder.

genetic engineering The transfer of a gene from the DNA of one organism into another organism, in order to produce an organism with desired traits.

GLOSSARY

genome The complete set of genetic information that an organism carries in its DNA.

germination The sprouting of the embryo out of a seed; occurs when the embryo resumes its growth following dormancy.

gland An organ that produces and releases chemicals either through ducts or into the bloodstream.

H

habitat An environment that provides the things a specific organism needs to live, grow, and reproduce.

heredity The passing of traits from parents to offspring.

heterotroph An organism that cannot make its own food and gets food by consuming other living things.

homeostasis The condition in which an organism's internal environment is kept stable in spite of changes in the external environment.

homologous structures Structures that are similar in different species and that have been inherited from a common ancestor.

hormone The chemical produced by an endocrine gland.; A chemical that affects growth and development.

host An organism that provides a source of energy or a suitable environment for a parasite to live with, in, or on.

I

inheritance The process by which an offspring receives genes from its parents.

instinct A response to a stimulus that is inborn.

invasive species Species that are not native to a habitat and can out-compete native species in an ecosystem.

invertebrate An animal without a backbone.

K

keystone species A species that influences the survival of many other species in an ecosystem.

L

limiting factor An environmental factor that causes a population to decrease in size.

lymph Fluid that travels through the lymphatic system consisting of water, white blood cells, and dissolved materials.

M

mammal A vertebrate whose body temperature is regulated by its internal heat, and that has skin covered with hair or fur and glands that produce milk to feed its young.

mating system Behavior patterns related to how animals mate.

mechanism The natural process by which something takes place.

migration The regular, seasonal journey of an animal from one place to another and back again.

mitochondria Rod-shaped organelles that convert energy in food molecules to energy the cell can use to carry out its functions.

molecule A group of small, nonliving particles that make up all material.

multicellular Consisting of many cells.

mutation Any change in the DNA of a gene or a chromosome.

mutualism A type of symbiosis in which both species benefit from living together.

N

natural resource Anything naturally occurring in the environment that humans use.

natural selection The process by which organisms that are best adapted to their environment are most likely to survive and reproduce.

negative feedback A process in which a system is turned off by the condition it produces.

nephron Small filtering structure found in the kidneys that removes wastes from blood and produces urine.

neuron A cell that carries information through the nervous system.

nucleus In cells, a large oval organelle that contains the cell's genetic material in the form of DNA and controls many of the cell's activities.

nutrients Substances in food that provide the raw materials and energy needed for an organism to carry out its essential processes.

O

organ A body structure that is composed of different kinds of tissues that work together.

organ system A group of organs that work together to perform a major function.

organelle A tiny cell structure that carries out a specific function within the cell.

organism A living thing.

osmosis The diffusion of water molecules across a selectively permeable membrane.

ovule A plant structure in seed plants that produces the female gametophyte; contains an egg cell.

P

parasite An organism that benefits by living with, on, or in a host in a parasitism interaction.

parasitism A type of symbiosis in which one organism lives with, on, or in a host and harms it.

peristalsis Waves of smooth muscle contractions that move food through the esophagus toward the stomach.

pheromone A chemical released by one animal that affects the behavior of another animal of the same species.

photoperiodism A plant's response to seasonal changes in the length of night and day.

photosynthesis The process by which plants and other autotrophs capture and use light energy to make food from carbon dioxide and water.

pioneer species The first species to populate an area during succession.

pollination The transfer of pollen from male reproductive structures to female reproductive structures in plants.

population All the members of one species living in the same area.

precipitation Any form of water that falls from clouds and reaches Earth's surface as rain, snow, sleet, or hail.

predation An interaction in which one organism kills another for food or nutrients.

probability A number that describes how likely it is that a particular event will occur.

producer An organism that can make its own food.

protein Large organic molecule made of carbon, hydrogen, oxygen, nitrogen, and sometimes sulfur.

protist A eukaryotic organism that cannot be classified as an animal, plant, or fungus.

R

recessive allele An allele that is hidden whenever the dominant allele is present.

reflex An automatic response that occurs rapidly and without conscious control.

response An action or change in behavior that occurs as a result of a stimulus.

S

saliva A fluid produced in the mouth that aids in mechanical and chemical digestion.

scientific theory A well-tested explanation for a wide range of observations or experimental results.

selectively permeable A property of cell membranes that allows some substances to pass across it, while others cannot.

sex chromosomes The pair of chromosomes carrying genes that determine whether a person is biologically male or female.

sex-linked gene A gene carried on a sex chromosome.

sexual reproduction A reproductive process that involves two parents that combine their genetic material to produce a new organism which differs from both parents.

species A group of similar organisms that can mate with each other and produce offspring that can also mate and reproduce.

GLOSSARY

spinal cord A thick column of nervous tissue that links the brain to nerves in the body.

spontaneous generation The mistaken idea that living things arise from nonliving sources.

stimulus Any change or signal in the environment that can make an organism react in some way.

stress The reaction of a person's body to potentially threatening, challenging, or disturbing events.

succession The series of predictable changes that occur in a community over time.

sustainability The ability of an ecosystem to maintain bioviersity and production indefinitely.

symbiosis Any relationship in which two species live closely together and that benefits at least one of the species.

synapse The junction where one neuron can transfer an impulse to the next structure.

T

tissue A group of similar cells that perform a specific function.

trait A specific characteristic that an organism can pass to its offspring through its genes.

tropism A plant's growth response toward or away from a stimulus.

U

unicellular Made of a single cell.

V

vaccine A substance used in a vaccination that consists of pathogens that have been weakened or killed but can still trigger the body to produce chemicals that destroy the pathogens.

vacuole A sac-like organelle that stores water, food, and other materials.

variation Any difference between individuals of the same species.

vein A blood vessel that carries blood back to the heart.

vertebrate An animal with a backbone.

virus A tiny, nonliving particle that enters and then reproduces inside a living cell.

INDEX

INDEX

CREDITS

Photography

Photo locators denoted as follows: Top (T), Center (C), Bottom (B), Left (L), Right (R), Background (Bkgrd)

Covers

Front: Don Johnston/All Canada Photos/Getty Images; Back: Marinello/DigitalVision Vectors/Getty Images

Instructional Segment 4

iv: Nick Lundgren/Shutterstock; vi: Tonyz20/Shutterstock; viii: Kelly vanDellen/Alamy Stock Photo; viii: Fabriziobalconi/Fotolia; ixBkgrd: Brian J. Skerry/National Geographic/Getty Images; ixB: Dale Kolke/ZUMA Press/Newscom; 004T: Sabena Jane Blackbird/Alamy Stock Photo; 004C: Sinclair Stammers/Science Source; 004B: Science Stock Photography/Science Source; 005T: Georg Gerster/Science Source; 005B: The Natural History Museum/Alamy Stock Photo; 006T: GL Archive/Alamy Stock Photo; 006B: Brian J. Skerry/Getty Images; 008-009: Tonyz20/Shutterstock; 009: MarcelClemens/Shutterstock; 010-011: Blickwinkel/Alamy Stock Photo; 012-013: Jo Crebbin/Shutterstock; 013: Loop Images Ltd/Alamy Stock Photo; 014: Fototeca Gilardi/akg-images; 016T: Holmes Garden Photos/Alamy Stock Photo; 016B: Russell Shively/Shutterstock; 018L: Westend61/Getty Images; 018R: Brian Kushner/Alamy Stock Photo; 022-023: Visual China Group/Getty Images; 024L: Nature Photographers Ltd/Alamy Stock Photo; 024C: Pises Tungittipokai/Shutterstock; 024R: Oli Scarff/AFP/Getty Images; 025: Nature Photographers Ltd/Alamy Stock Photo; 026: IrinaK/Shutterstock; 028: Kali9/Getty Images; 029L: Zeljko Radojko/Shutterstock; 029R: Patricia Isaza; 030: IrinaK/Shutterstock; 031T: All Canada Photos/Alamy Stock Photo; 031B: REUTERS/Ulises Rodriguez/Alamy Stock Photo; 032-033: imageBROKER/Alamy Stock Photo; 036T: Angel DiBilio/Shutterstock; 036C: Bazzano Photography/Alamy Stock Photo; 036B: Sailorr/Shutterstock; 038-039: Martin Shields/Alamy Stock Photo; 039: Vodolaz/Fotolia; 040L: YAY Media AS/Alamy Stock Photo; 040R: Wwing/Getty Images; 041L: The Science Picture Company/Alamy Stock Photo; 041C: Fabian von Poser/Getty Images; 041R: Scott Camazine/Alamy Stock Photo; 042: Bildagentur Zoonar GmbH/Shutterstock; 044L: Pedro Bernardo/Shutterstock; 044R: Steve Vidler/Alamy Stock Photo; 047T: Barry Mansell/Nature Picture Library; 047B: Michelle Gilders/Alamy Stock Photo; 048T: Francois Gohier/VWPics/Alamy Stock Photo; 048BL: Mark Carwardine/Getty Images; 048BR: Wolfgang Pölzer/Alamy Stock Photo; 050-051: WaterFrame/Alamy Stock Photo; 055: Abeselom Zerit/Shutterstock; 057T: BGSmith/Shutterstock; 057B: Don Johnston/Getty Images; 060L: Gallinago_media/Shutterstock; 060R: CLS Digital Arts/Shutterstock; 061: J Hindman/Shutterstock; 067L: Moose henderson/Shutterstock; 067R: iStock/Getty Images.

Take Notes

Use this space for recording notes and sketching out ideas.

Take Notes

Use this space for recording notes and sketching out ideas.

Use this space for recording notes and sketching out ideas.

Take Notes

Use this space for recording notes and sketching out ideas.